THE ROSE+CROSS

A Rosicrucian Insight Into
Contemporary Inner Development

Olivier Manitara

THE ROSE + CROSS

A Rosicrucian Insight Into
Contemporary Inner Development

Brotherhood-Sisterhood Press

With the love inside the rose of the heart, I dedicate this book to all of the students of the Christi Brotherhood-Sisterhood of the Rose+Cross, all around the world, who work within the temple of the Holy Spirit for the luminous renewal of life on earth.

To all those who, upon approaching our sacred mysteries, have felt themselves becoming better people, and have decided to work for the good of all beings, under the auspices of the highest-conceived light.

Olivier Manitara

Brotherhood-Sisterhood Press is an imprint of
Telesma-Evida Publishing
P.O. Box 174, Ahuntsic
Montreal (Qc) H3L 3N7, Canada

2/01

Canadian Cataloguing in Publication Data

Manitara, Olivier, 1964-
The Rose + Cross : a Rosicrucian insight
into contemporary inner development

Translation of: La Rose + Croix.
ISBN 1-894341-02-3

221 p.

1. Rosicrucians. I. Title.

BF1623.R7M2513 1999   135'.43   C99-901214-2

Legal deposit fourth quarter 1999
National Library of Canada
National Library of Quebec

CONTENTS

THE LIVING AND MODERN
MESSAGE OF THE ROSE+CROSS

A BASIC INTRODUCTION TO
THE TEACHINGS OF THE ROSE+CROSS

THE CHRISTIANITY
OF THE ROSE+CROSS

THE CIRCLE OF LIGHT
OF THE COSMIC TRADITION

THE INNER EXPERIENCES OF
A STUDENT OF THE MODERN ROSE+CROSS

THE MEANING OF LIFE

Dear Friends-Readers,

Although he respects all of them, the author has no ties to any physically constituted organization of the Rose+Cross, and he does not owe his initiation to any one of them. He draws his knowledge from the invisible source of the mystical and scientific Order.

Brotherhood-Sisterhood Press is happy to participate actively in the propagation of the modern message of the eternal wisdom.

We thank all of our readers for their confidence. We hope that you will enjoy reading this work and that you will find it to be a source of new inspiration and inner development.

Brotherhood-Sisterhood Press

The light of true wisdom is
the consecration which changes
the physical man into a true man in the spirit.
The spiritual sun of wisdom carries
within itself the image of the true man,
which shows the disciple how man
should be, how man was conceived
by God in perfection and purity.

The Living and Modern Message of the Rose+Cross

Dear Reader,

Many books have been published all over the world about the Rose+Cross, and so you might ask: "Why one more?" Can this ancient mystical Order bring something truly positive to our modern society?

The Rose+Cross has a long past, but is still alive in the present, and its message of light and of great hope for humanity is perfectly suited to contemporary life. This universal message is the way to salvation; it must, therefore, always accompany humanity along its path, and remain accessible to anyone who aspires to know it, who wishes to have a better life—healthier and more constructive.

Whether we want to or not, we spend the greatest part of our existence with ourselves. People live within their interior being, and often society is a way for them to try to escape from themselves. People refuse to meet themselves, to become aware, and to expand their inner reality; but, no matter where they hide, they cannot escape from themselves. The Rose+Cross rises above trends and societies because it is interested in what is eternal in the human being and in the world. It invites us to meet ourselves, in our own nature, and to restore order within ourselves. When this order—the Cross— has been established within us, it radiates harmony; we feel good, and experience a state of peace and joy. It is then that the Rose appears; our soul opens up and begins to speak to us, and we experience our true identity.

Such an experience is absolutely not in opposition to con-temporary life. On the contrary, it allows one to find the strength to enrich society and, above all, to give it a new and clearer meaning, better understood by people—those who are no longer hiding from themselves.

Therefore, this book is not historical in the sense of an external analysis; rather, it flows from the inner source of the mystical Brotherhood-Sisterhood. It focuses on that which is living and present, as possibilities for the renewal of modern humanity.

It is clear that, in order to stay awake, we often need to take a fresh look at ourselves and our own lives. Constructive questioning and self-analysis are as important to our health as washing our bodies or cleaning the house. But, to be truly new, this look has to come from above, from the source of the universal spirit. It is the task of the Rose+Cross to bring this new perspective to the world and to send cyclical calls to humanity, to warn it in a free and friendly way.

This is a fundamental law, on which a great deal of meditating is required: we are not aware of the things which surround us in our everyday lives. For example, we are hardened to the suffering, the atrocities and the absurdities which are so present in our lives. We find them normal; we have accepted them and we no longer see them. The first time a child sees its grandmother cutting the throat of a rabbit to eat, it may be frightened to see so much cruelty in a person it thought it knew. But the grandmother finds this activity perfectly normal, and it does not take the child long to get used to it.

In the same way, an extraterrestrial, coming from the realm of kindness, love, harmony, and self-mastery to study the world of humans, would be shocked by so much suffering, hate, absurdity, etc.—whereas, for humans, this is all normal.

People accept all this because they are cut off from looking at the world in the way which comes from the world of the universal spirit.

We have also become accustomed to hearing about the

Rose+Cross. The existence of a holy gathering of light no longer surprises us. We think we know all about it—yet our lives do not change. The Rose+Cross does not wish to encourage the old and false conceptions that people have of the world, but, instead, to give them the fresh perspective of a child— allowing them to discover what is before their eyes and to become aware of the source of the suffering and atrocities which are, more and more, part of everyday life.

The Rose+Cross brings to humanity the great remedy, the great healing.

This involves a fundamental, universal reformation—both internal and external; and, therefore, only the bravest, the most aware and the most daring can hear the call of the light. During the time of the Master Jesus, only the most valiant and intrepid dared to meet him and follow him—sometimes even in secret, like Nicodemus—because it was extremely dangerous, forbidden by law.

As soon as he died, everybody started to claim him; they instituted a church and dogmas, monopolizing his words and using them to their own advantage.

However, the Master is not dead, and the Rose+Cross is not an institution established and claimed by the world. It is alive, and continues still, at the present moment, to invite people to know themselves and to act in the right way.

So take a look at yourself, and really look at the world in a new way, founded on the basic state of peace and serenity; and you will discover new possibilities in life.

This book is not a novel, but emanates from an esoteric teaching. It must, therefore, be read with the attentive and awakened state of mind of one who seeks.

Everything that is esoteric, internal, secret, pertaining to the future of humanity, is extremely difficult to explain and understand. All that is familiar is easy to understand, but that which is new always demands effort if we are to absorb it. That is why it is a good idea to have intermittent moments of silence as you read, so that the soul can be touched and calmly absorb the teachings.

These teachings contain many meanings in differing degrees of consciousness. That is why they are meant to be deepened by meditation.

This book is written for those who have an open mind and a heart which is ready to love and to be re-born, and who feel that they are part of the global family of the well-intentioned.

On earth, there is a real communion of souls among all well-intentioned people, and it is to them that the words of the invisible Brotherhood-Sisterhood of the contemporary Rose+Cross are addressed. It is this Brotherhood-Sisterhood which stands by all loving hearts, ready to support them and to give the liberating impulse which allows for the achievement of good.

The Brotherhood-Sisterhood of light tells the family of those who are well-intentioned:

"Open up to the wisdom, to the love and to the truth that are coming into the world here and now, in a new way.

Cultivate the limitless force of good and enter into the vibration of conscious work for the benefit of All, following the will of your most sacred inner being.

Open that door which is in front of you and which has been closed for thousands of years; you will be surprised to discover a distant and infinite world stretching out in front of you. Thus, that which is close, that which is within reach of your hand, will allow you to understand and commune with the endless universe."

All you have to do is open the door to perceive that, behind everything that is limited, there exists a limitless world. You have this experience every day when you leave your home.

Many people pass by the universal Brotherhood-Sisterhood of those who are enlightened by God without seeing it, without paying attention, because the doors to their souls are closed.

This book wishes to speak to your soul so that you can discover what is hidden within it.

Only an awakened soul can discover the soul of another.

Only an awakened soul can open the door and start to live the new life of the infinite world.

Ignorant people can pray for hours
for an end to war in the world,
while finding it normal to remain
at war within themselves.

A Basic Introduction to the Teachings of the Rose+Cross

The Call of the Rose and the Way of the Cross

In considering the question of the sacred Brotherhood-Sisterhood of the Rose+Cross, we touch upon one of the most magnificent, elevated and essential subjects concerning humanity and its history.

If feelings of respect, admiration and silence rise up within you at the mere mention of the name of the holy gathering of light, then open your ears and be welcome to these pages, because they were written for you.

Just a few whiffs of the perfume of the sweetheart can fill the soul of the lover with tender memories and the secret joy of being able to see their loved one again.

The Rose+Cross also gives off a fragrance, a subtle resonance, which can touch the deepest realms of human goodness and lead the aspirant through the sacred gates to our eternal mysteries.

The lover is filled with wonder, transported, ennobled by the beauty of the loved one; yet no beauty can compare to the Rose+Cross, which is its source. The Rose calls humanity to the supreme bliss, the happiness, the fullness for which everybody is looking. Art which evokes immortal and infinite beauty is the most powerful stimulant for the regeneration of the spirit. In this way, all beings hear the call to happiness, but few are those who find the right path to it, the one which leads straight to the goal: the path of the Cross.

Humans cannot live without beauty, and all that beautifies life is an emanation from the great Sun of Truth. Beauty is found in the elevation of the mind and is realized on earth through the Cross. The path of the Rose+Cross is one of beauty and work, to enrich life in every way. And so the Rose of perfect beauty finds its place on the Cross of work and sacrifice.

When the beauty of the mind manifests itself on earth through art, life finds itself magnified and lifted up to a higher vibration.

The Rose tells us of supreme love and the Cross reminds us

of the usefulness of wisdom in life on the earth. That is why Apuleius, in his novel *The Golden Ass*, explains to us that a donkey cannot get close to roses. It is not good to approach love without wisdom, because that often leads to great distress. On the other hand, the union of the greatest love with the most penetrating wisdom gives birth to truth, from which comes liberty.

A person who makes a mistake in love suffers, and that suffering is transformed by time into wisdom, which shows them where true love is, where they can find supreme happiness.

It is life which leads people to the Rose+Cross, because it is the symbol of the true man, of what human beings must become in order to be fulfilled.

To those who have eyes to see, the Rose reveals the indescribable beauty of the future man, of the perfect man, and the Cross shows the way to the tests and the struggles—the path of initiation. So only the vision of the beauty of the spirit allows one to find the strength needed to accomplish their task on earth and to triumph over the obstacles of doubt and despair which hinder evolution.

The concepts of evolution and ascension are the keys to the wisdom of the Cross, which allows us to triumph over destruction.

The Rule of the Order

Many renowned thinkers, people of science and of the heart, have tried to enter the temple of the mysteries of the Brotherhood-Sisterhood of the light of God and of Goodness without success. They reached only the periphery of the invisible Order, but were still able to receive medical, economic, political and scientific secrets—which are now part of our society.

That all these discoveries are not officially recognized as being inspired by the enlightened Brothers and Sisters of the Rose✠Cross is intentional, because the rule of the Order is to offer its deeds only to God, the success and fame to another person, and the work to oneself.

The Rose✠Cross works only according to the will of God, which is known to them. They receive this knowledge by opening up the rose of the heart, an initiatic method, following the words of Christ: *"Blessed are they who are pure of heart, for they shall see God."*

The Rose✠Cross is at one with these other words of Christ: *"Father, not my will, but Your will be done."*

For them, these words are like a light in which they always remain. This is not a belief, a dogma or a wish, but a state of being which they have attained. For this reason, we can say that they offer their deeds solely to God, who is a real, living presence in their hearts.

Then they offer their success, the fruit of their constant work, to another to protect the anonymity, the invisibility, of the Community. In this way, they apply the words of Christ:

"Refrain from practicing your justice in front of people to be noticed by them, or you will receive no reward from your Father in heaven.

When you give alms, do not ring the bell before you, like the hypocrites in the churches and the streets, to be glorified by others. In truth, I tell you, they already have their reward.

When you give alms, do not let your left hand know what your right hand is doing, so that your alms may be done in secret; then your Father, who sees in secret, will reward you."

For the Rose+Cross, "giving alms" means working for the good of all beings according to the will of God. And we can clearly state here that all that is truly beneficial in humanity comes through them, for they are the source of goodness on our planet.

The Universal Reform

The Brotherhood-Sisterhood never stops working for the healthy and harmonious evolution of humanity. For a while, the world hears nothing about it, as it is working intensely in secret.

Then it manifests itself physically—to heal, to comfort and to help humanity more directly. For example, in 1600, it showed itself in Europe, inviting all the greatest thinkers to rally round its cause for universal reform.

In feudal times, the Brotherhood-Sisterhood addressed both princes and peasants in the same direct way, on the same level. It insisted on the importance of education for all, so that all people could be freed from ignorance and superstition. It established the foundations of democracy and modern science. Virtually all the greatest scientists, philosophers and inventors to whom we owe so much were either directly or indirectly linked to the Rose+Cross.

It whispered into people's minds the first ideas for the realization of the United States of Europe and a universal brotherhood-sisterhood among all peoples, based on mutual cooperation.

All these ideas, which are still current today, were already the objectives of the Rose+Cross in the 16th Century. This can be verified if history is studied objectively, without prejudice, in the light of what we are revealing.

The conclusion to all these facts is that people have no idea of the forces that direct their destiny and push them forward. It is therefore necessary that an awakening, in this sense, take place, because: *"When the blind lead the blind, they are all in danger of falling into a hole."*

That is why the modern Rose+Cross is sending out a new appeal to those who want to, and are able to, hear it: *"It is of crucial importance to our era that man be able to awaken to the knowledge of his true self and to purity, in an individual and conscious way, to distinguish clearly the external and internal influences which make him take action, and thereby to lay the foundations for his development and his destiny, in a healthy and healing way."*

The Secrets of the Rose+Cross

The fact that the Rose+Cross is an initiatic community, secret and impenetrable, has been misunderstood. Many esoteric books were written and movements were created using its name, taking advantage of the attraction of mystery. In this way, many true things became mixed up with the untrue. Today some historians are trying to sort it all out. But one must understand that only members of the Brotherhood-Sisterhood truly know what is inside its gates; and they cannot speak of it, even if they want to. The others—those who are on the outside—can only theorize and make assumptions.

Never have the secrets of the Rose+Cross been completely divulged on the outside, because the world is not ready to hear them or to receive them in the correct way. If those secrets were given to the world, it would mean that the day of the Most Holy One had arrived, that Jerusalem was descending from the heavens, that the kingdom of God and the Solar Culture were about to be realized.

The Brothers and Sisters respect the sayings of their Master:

"Broken secrets lose their value;

Desecration destroys Grace;

Do not throw pearls before swine;

And do not make a bed of roses for a donkey."

Mystery attracts, surprises, and stimulates the curiosity; or irritates and awakens the negative tendencies of the ego, which feels left out. There is a certain type of mind in the world that does not like mystery, and that tries hard to make us believe that it does not exist, that science has rational answers to all questions.

Even though it was the Rose+Cross that laid the foundations for reason and scientific method, its aim was to unite science with the mysteries of life. There is something sacred, divine, in mystery—something which comes from the opening of the heart. The desire to suppress mystery is a negative attitude which reveals the presence of the enemy of humanity. The desire to penetrate the mysteries of life with a respectful and just attitude is a method which ennobles one and lifts one up into the light.

So the school of Hierophants of the Rose+Cross remains secret, closed, and impenetrable to the wicked, the cruel, liars, traitors, swine, and manipulators of the human conscience.

The only way to know it is to be called by it directly, after having shown oneself to be worthy and able by one's eagerness to serve humanity and the great force of good in purity.

Horizontality and Verticality

The Rose+Cross works in two directions: horizontality and verticality.

Through horizontality, it transmits creative and renewing impulses to humanity so that it will evolve in the right way. Everyone of kind heart and intelligence is contacted to take part in this task.

Through verticality, it sends out a call for individual initiation, and another force comes into play. Difficult trials are sent to man throughout his life (most of the time, he does not understand that these are tests), and he must triumph over them.

Those who aspire to individual initiation should meditate carefully on the legend of the witch Circe, who turned Ulysses' companions into pigs by making them drink from the cup of

THE ROSE+CROSS

the pleasures of life.

There are two ways to approach the Rose of Beauty; there are those who monopolize and defile it, and those who wish to use it as a springboard to the realm of the spirit. These two approaches show us two different types of life. One understands the mystery of the Cross; the other does not. One thinks only of enjoying life, and the other only of serving it. One turns into a pig, while the other embarks on the enriching path of light.

The Fire of Ideal Beauty

The Brotherhood-Sisterhood of light is not against joy or the pleasures of life—quite the contrary. That is why it chose the rose as its emblem. It is good to love life and to be open to all its pleasures—at least, to those that do not damage health. But you must not stop there; otherwise, it means that the universe was created only for people's pleasure. Life is a gift; life is wonderful. That is true, but you yourself must also become a gift and a treasure for the universe, because only in this way can there be a mutual and harmonious exchange.

This is an absolute rule for the disciples of the Rose+Cross. They are not cut off from the many impressions of life, but they transform them into the light of wisdom so that they can offer

38

them to the universe as an evolving force.

Thanks to the strength of idealism which lives in them, they are able to take the raw material (pleasure) and turn it into a work of art. The artist is a creator inspired by the fire of ideal beauty which burns within. In this way, one forces nature to submit to one's own law, that of the spirit, just as Ulysses subjugated the sorceress Circe, using his sword and the superior mystical force which inhabited his soul.

The Cross tells us of the reality of the world and the Rose invites us to the ideal vision of the beauty of the spirit. That which is beautiful and sublime can radiate within the soul and thus provide the force to triumph over the inevitability of death, by giving a taste, through sacred art, of ineffable eternity.

It is a fundamental law that the light of idealism which comes from the contemplation of the distant world, of the world beyond form, generates a sublimation, an ennoblement, a sanctification of the everyday—just as sunlight beautifies a landscape or an object.

In every human being, there is a light similar to the sun. Without it, everything becomes dark, cold and sad. If it shines and radiates, everything becomes beautiful, enthusiastic, joyful, sublime, magnificent. The sun is the greatest artist of all, and the Brothers and Sisters of the Rose+Cross are its closest disciples.

The one who looks only at the everyday, external realities of life, who is satisfied passively to receive ideas, information and feelings, without finding a superior ideal force within—which can enrich everything and open the gates of wisdom, which gives meaning and love, which realizes the divine—that one is, with every breath, allowing their soul to die a little more.

Idealistic and Mystical Art

If you aspire to enter the gate of initiation, you must awaken your soul by way of everything that surrounds it. It is not good to live in the world like an empty shell, because a person is great only when they have noble and beautiful ideas, and an absolute confidence that good will always triumph. This ideal vision of the world of beauty is not innate; it has to be consciously cultivated. That is the work of the candidate for initiation, of the disciple.

The holy gathering of the Rose+Cross cultivates the secret science of idealistic and mystical art, as a way of ennobling man.

Using those who carry within themselves such a spiritual perception of the distant world of infinite beauty, etheric forces of healing and renewal can flow on earth and in humanity. This is the mark of our Brotherhood-Sisterhood.

For a man who has developed this clearness of vision in his soul, the ravishing body of a woman becomes a way to rise towards the beauty of the soul and to discover a superior method of creation, to receive revelations and inspirations of the spirit. But, for a man who is devoid of such an ideal perception, the woman—even the most beautiful—is no more than a means to satisfy a need. He turns into a pig.

Everything in the Rose speaks to us of delicacy, of refinement, of subtlety, of beauty, and of elevation. It is the messenger of divine mercy, which, by way of its intermediary, opens the gate of salvation for those who are obliged to carry the Cross of everyday life and suffering on their backs. The force of habit, of routine, is the greatest trap along the path, because it puts the soul to sleep.

For the student of the Rose+Cross, every part of their daily life must be studied, purified and ennobled by the mystical and idealistic force of their soul. This work is described by the Master and instructor of our venerable Order as "the study of the *Liber Mundi*—the study of the book of the world."

In those moments of silence and great calm which the disciple knows he must give himself, he tries consciously to rise towards the idea of grandeur and beauty which exists in everything. In fact, in every area, he always searches for the highest idea and the most profound perception; and then he makes every effort to act, using this as his starting point.

For the wise person, the simplest situation is an occasion to reveal wisdom.

For the artist, the most ordinary scenes conceal a hidden beauty.

For Truth, all is truth.

For Love, all is love.

And, for the "pig", everything is an opportunity to wallow in filth and make life dirty.

The Enemies of the Rose+Cross

All of this means that the Order of the Rose+Cross is not invisible to those who have pure hearts, to souls searching for wisdom, and for those who love God and that which is the highest, the greatest, the most beautiful.

Likewise, the spirit of the Order can be seen in the world through everything that is noble, good and sacred, and that manifests itself as an impulse aiming to liberate the image of the true man, and to make it evolve.

Therefore, the Rose+Cross should absolutely not be taken for a fashionable club. Many people, learning of the existence of our Brotherhood-Sisterhood, have wished to be part of it because it has an air of mystery about it. It can be considered very "chic" to belong to such a group; it can boost the ego. One can suddenly feel important by having a membership card from the order of the *Rosae+Crucis*. But it is very clear that such an attitude has nothing to do with the real Rose+Cross. However, this attitude was taken seriously by many people; and it caused much harm to, and many illusions about, the mission of the Brothers and Sisters beloved by God.

The enemies of humanity used all this to make trouble and to turn minds away from the great goal. This did so much harm that the expression "Loved by God" is no longer understood at all by modern people, like all the expressions used to describe the Rose+Cross.

Some people, understanding that the holy gathering was closed to them, because of their deep-rooted baseness, turned against it and tried to attack it, to dirty its name by all possible means, and to close its doors, so that others would not be able to enter its bosom and be raised up into the light of the true man.

It is natural that those who have this baseness within themselves, and who do not wish to change, should want to drag others down to their level, so that no one will notice that they are dominated by an inferior and egoistical nature.

The closer human beings get to their true divine nature, in purity, by contrast, the more the other side of their nature— the inferior side—becomes visible within them. A vice cannot pass unseen when surrounded by virtue, but it certainly can when surrounded by other vices! This is how some people have cultivated, and still cultivate, baseness in their fellow man, in order to prevent him from gaining access to heaven— a place they themselves feel incapable of reaching.

If you have eyes to see, then look; take the time to verify, by yourself, without prejudice, and be wary of the advice of baseness.

The Awakening of Logical Understanding

This is the great method of the Rose+Cross for awakening conscious discernment in each individual—the force of logic. Through logic, man is able to recognize the truth in the Rosicrucian teachings. But he must study objectively, stripped of all vanity, passion, fear, laziness, and prejudice. He must cultivate in his soul a state of profound serenity and a pure aspiration for truth.

Those who have achieved this state of being are ready to study our wisdom. They have climbed the first step of the temple of the Holy Spirit. On the other hand, those who have not achieved this level of logical and objective reasoning are not ready to receive the shining rays of the truth into their minds. When such persons receive the truth, they can only profane and distort it.

For us, the human being is an instrument capable of perceiving truth, just like the microscope or the telescope for the scientist. If the instrument is not regulated correctly or is not working properly, the image will be distorted beyond remedy. This is a logical understanding of an initiatic phenomenon concerning the ennoblement of man. This logical observation can be verified in theory, but also in practice, for Rosicrucian teaching always leads to a transformation, an improvement of life. That is its goal.

The Order's external science has led to the improvement of physical life in an extraordinary way, but it can also improve the inner life, in an even more extraordinary manner.

That which is true is true, and can therefore be verified, in a rational manner, in all worlds—the spiritual as well as the physical. Truth is afraid of nothing, and only dishonesty can deny it and disguise it.

The Rose+Cross does not appeal to that which is dishonest, but only to the objective intelligence of its future students. This Rosicrucian method of teaching has been copied in western schools and universities, and is now spreading all over the world. The only problem is that materialistic scientists and teachings stayed with the study of tangible facts but did not expand the method to include the spiritual world. Therefore, even the world of objective facts was closed to them and they developed the same dishonesty for which they had originally denounced the catholic church and other dogmatic religions.

The Instructors and Guides of the Holy Brotherhood-Sisterhood

Therefore, all those with reasonable and logical minds can understand and absorb the teaching of the Rose+Cross. This shows a veritable evolution in initiation because, before, and especially in the oriental tradition, the only way to gain access to the path of spiritual ascension was to have faith in the *guru*. The disciple was never asked to understand anything, but just to have faith in the Master. The greater the faith and devotion, the faster the disciple progressed.

In the Rose+Cross Brotherhood-Sisterhood of western mysteries, there is no *guru* in the religious sense of the word. There are Masters, instructors who guide the students as school teachers would. These beings have acquired a certain knowledge, an inner experience and realization, which they convey to their students in a natural way.

The truth taught by the Rose+Cross is true in and of itself, and everyone can have access to it in a free and independent way by using the right methods. The first thing that the students have to learn is to think for themselves; and that is not easy, and requires a long apprenticeship. The study of mathematics can help one to achieve this logical thinking. Mathematics is true by itself, independently of the teacher. When students have learned science from the professor, they can teach it, too—and even be better than their teacher. This is what Christ meant when he said: *"The one who follows my teaching will be able to do what I do, and even more."*

So the Rose+Cross is a real, spiritual Brotherhood-Sisterhood of sincere friends who commune at the same source of science, of love, and of beauty, for the good and the free perfecting of all beings. But you should not believe that the Brotherhood-Sisterhood is simply a union of utopian philosophers who study among themselves for their own satisfaction. The enlightened Brothers and Sisters are people of action, builders and healers in every field.

If you enter the Brotherhood-Sisterhood's circle of light, know that your work for the good, whatever it is, will never be lost, because the Brothers and Sisters work without respite throughout the centuries.

The Obstacle of Blind Faith

Now I must say a little more about logical thought and the Rose+Cross method. Over the centuries, it is clear that the Brotherhood-Sisterhood has, by many different means, made a great effort to enable individuals to think more and more for themselves, to form an opinion by using their own intelligence, together with reason.

On the other hand, a large number of people have romanti-cized and sensationalized the Rosicrucian teaching, and the spiritual world, which is one method among many. (As an aside, it must be recognized that, when talking about the Brotherhood-Sisterhood, what is wondrous about it goes far beyond what has been said.) However, this approach is absolutely not in accord with our venerable Order, because the romanticized description of one's own spiritual experience can only arouse in the reader a feeling of faith or rejection.

The Brotherhood-Sisterhood has always been suspicious of a spirituality that is purely sentimental, without wisdom and concrete actions. A blind faith has been accorded to the authority of hypothetical and invisible "Masters", while the real work, and the visible and genuine Masters of the Rose+Cross have been neglected. People prefer the world of sentimental pleasure to that of concrete reality, which demands effort and serious questioning.

If, under the cover of spirituality, someone is looking for a selfish thrill, an esoteric reassurance, then it is very clear that he is not ready for initiation and real work.

We, too, could have described our meetings with the Brotherhood-Sisterhood of light, and made a showy display of all that is wondrous and marvelous; but that is absolutely not in agreement with the ethic of our venerable Order. It is much more sane and helpful to present principles, laws and firm facts that can be understood by everyone with logical reasoning. So the students keep their freedom; they can walk on the path, seeking to make their own discoveries through their own experiences.

One of the negative consequences of romanticizing the teachings is that it makes people project their thoughts towards an imaginary world, where they are introduced to "Masters" who have no relevance to daily earthly reality.

The fact is that the Brothers and Sisters of the genuine Rose+Cross have endured and still endure all of the miseries, obstacles and sufferings of everyday life; and it is only because they find the strength to overcome and transcend them that they become great, men in the full sense of the word.

Know that the real Masters and the guides of humanity were just like you, and that they often become so again to help their followers. So, your daily life and the circumstances in which you find yourself are not obstacles on the path which leads to our art.

The Necessity of Experiencing the Teaching For Yourself

A real candidate must not try to make excuses, but, rather, they must look for the hand of God, the profound inner significance of everything that surrounds them. It is then that they will perceive the purpose of all that they are called to live through;

and no longer will poverty or wealth be an obstacle to their progression in divine service.

Those who complain about external circumstances prove, by that fact, that they are dominated by events and that it is not the creative power of their awakened soul that has the upper hand and is in charge of the situation. The Brotherhood-Sisterhood of the Rose+Cross is not content just to philosophize or to wish happiness to humanity, but works in a real way for good; and its students have to do the same, in whatever situation they find themselves.

Rosicrucian teaching, which is the true western spiritual teaching, can be received from the outside and understood by logical thought. For example, one can understand that love is better than hate, that peace is better than war, etc. One can philosophize about these questions and even come up with great theories, without ever experiencing love or peace, as a state of mind or being.

So we can talk about peace all our lives and continue to wage war at every turn.

The initiatic aspect of the Rose+Cross opens the door to living experience, which transforms the individual. Those who taste love as a state of mind are never the same again, and that is the real path; but it is not easy, and one must recognize and accept that fact.

It is easy to have great theories about love. Really loving—

allowing love to love through you, in purity—is difficult and even dangerous, because it is a living experience which transforms the whole being.

Therefore, our Brotherhood-Sisterhood has never romanticized, nor even described, the kingdom of light. It has always been content just to show the way, and to give the techniques which allow one to have the experience for oneself. Those who apply these methods under the protective guidance of experienced instructors will get results; there is no doubt about it.

Only a Rose+Cross Knows the Rose+Cross

The Brothers and Sisters of the august Brotherhood-Sisterhood of light have never done anything useless or unreasonable. Thus, they have not unveiled the mystery of their holy gathering, because, if one understands this mystery without being instantly transformed, then it is senseless, a grand illusion. Only the one who is a Rose+Cross knows the Rose+Cross; there is no other way. That is why they have always taught, in a sometimes veiled fashion, how to walk on the path of supreme good.

Dear friend on the path of life and maybe dear student, know that it is not possible to approach the great light of the Sun-Truth without being transformed, without giving yourself

THE ROSE+CROSS

in payment.

If you ask me: "What is the Rose+Cross?", I can give you a multitude of answers, but maybe the answer will kill the desire for knowledge. On the other hand, if I tell you: "Do this and you will discover it", then you begin the process of initiation, which leads you towards the perception of a higher, inner, living knowledge. Some seekers have not understood this fundamental law, and that is why the sacred Order of the *Rosae+Crucis* has remained invisible to them.

Dear seeker on the path, I have spoken to you from the depth of the rose of my heart; and I hope that you will find the supreme good in life: the treasure of light that is hidden within your soul.

We affirm the triumph of light,
the joy circulating in the holy community
of the well-intentioned, the comprehension of life
and the beauty of acting in cosmic unison.

The Christianity of the Rose+Cross

A Turning Point in Time

For a great part of humanity, the incarnation of Christ in the Master Jesus represented a turning point in world history.

This expression—"turning point in time"—is typically Rosicrucian because it contains a whole comprehension of the evolutionary march of humanity, of the earth, and of the cosmos, throughout time.

Humanity progresses in stages and certain moments are more important than others because they bring to fruition the efforts of an entire era and, at the same time, open up access to a new one.

The incarnation of Christ was one of these moments, and a great number of people did not hesitate to set time back to zero and to have history start with his birth on earth. It was clear to them that Christ would open up a new path to man; and this was verified by the blossoming of western civilization, which had been inspired by Christ and influenced by his close disciples: the Rose+Cross.

Making the history of humanity start with the incarnation of Christ shows to what extent the people of that time had perceived, in the events of Palestine, something vital to the evolution of humankind. One can say that people today have, for the most part, lost the great vision of the reality of Christ.

One gets the impression that the Christ presented to us by the churches is an ancient being who no longer fits into our modern civilization. But Rosicrucian Christianity has nothing to do with the current understanding of Christianity and the Christian religion.

It is totally adapted to modern life; it is even the inspiration and the source for it.

Without it, the tree of western civilization becomes rootless and begins, without fail, to rot and die.

The Universal Teaching of Christ

Christ's real teaching, that of the Rose+Cross and of the current of St. John, has never been understood, nor even transmitted to the world. It has been cultivated, in the greatest secrecy, through restricted circles of disciples, who have only offered the fruits of their discovery to the world, without ever revealing their origin.

That is how the Master wanted it, himself creating an outer circle, which could only receive the parable, and an inner circle, which participated directly in the mysteries of the kingdom of God. This inner circle has never disappeared; it has remained united with the being of Christ, and has traversed the ages, adapting the teaching to the new needs of humanity. This is how a gap, growing larger and larger, was formed between external Christianity, dogmatic and rigid, and the innovative, universal, living Christianity of the Rose+Cross.

It is necessary, in our times, that a great number of people be able to make contact with the Christianity of the Rose+Cross, in order to be better-equipped to face life, and to lay the solid foundations for a healthy and harmonious future. For it is through a real comprehension of the solar being of Christ that one can find the great reality of man. Without Christ, there is no man, in the real sense of the word, on earth. Without Christ, man loses his humanity. So Christ does not belong to a small group of pious people, but to all beings. Without him, no-one can truly blossom and evolve.

What the Master Jesus lived through in Palestine belongs to all men, and they must live through it during the course of their evolution. The Christ who manifested himself through the Master Jesus is a reality that exists in each human being, like conscience or breathing.

Thus, every being can live individually what the Master Jesus lived; everyone can experience within themselves the state of being and of mind, of Christ. This is the path of initiation, of rebirth. Human beings then become aware that, "alongside" the body and the mortal personality, there lives within an immortal state of being. The closer one gets to this state of being, the more is discovered the source of one's life, and of the life of all beings: the true being.

We are speaking here of something very intimate within the soul of man, and we want you to know that thousands of souls around the world have already lived this experience; these are the disciples of the current of St. John.

The Experience of St. Paul on the Road to Damascus

You, too, can live this kind of experience by entering this stream of light. Just as you were carried in your mother's body and came into the world, to make yourself a body and a personality, you can carry within yourself a superior state of consciousness, which does not come from the world, and which, by developing it, can lift you up into the light of the true being that you are eternally.

This is why St. Paul said: *"Already, it is no longer I who live, but Christ who lives in me."*

We have here a scientific experience. St. Paul was the declared enemy of Christ, until his spiritual eyes were opened and he discovered Christ before him in the soul of the world.

That is when he underwent a fundamental change of direction within himself, to the point of realizing that his mortal, perishable self was diminishing and his true human nature, Christ, was increasing.

St. Paul was led to live the same experience as the Master Jesus; Christ was living within him and he was aware of it. However, St. Paul was not a Master like Jesus or St. John; he had not yet mastered the three centers of the personality: thought, feeling and action.

One of the fundamental teachings of the Christians of the Rose+Cross is that any human being can have the same experience that St. Paul had on the road to Damascus, if they are correctly prepared. To demonstrate this fact, it is recounted that the Master and Guide of our Brotherhood-Sisterhood, Christian Rose+Cross, had the same experience on the road to Damascus.

The Awakening of the Rose of the Heart

Christ is a state of being of man that lives above the perishable personality and the lower nature, and everyone can get in touch with it. If the individual does not become aware of this state of being, then all their life they remain a prisoner of their lower nature, and do not know who they really are.

When the individual becomes aware of their divine nature, a great upheaval takes place; they have just been born into the spiritual world, they are no longer the same. They are like a new-born baby and must relearn everything: how to speak, to eat, to breathe, to move, etc. A new life appears before them; and, for them, time is set back to zero: Christ is reborn within their soul.

In the stream of St. John's humanity, this kind of rebirth has been called the "awakening of the rose of the heart".

Christ is the great principle of individualization. He reveals himself in that which can say: "I", "Myself", in the most intimate interior of the human soul. Christ is the source of the conscious "I". He is himself linked to the Source of sources: God, the supreme Being. That is why Christ has not only the power to give life to the mortal self of the earthly personality, but also to lift that self up into the light of the eternal soul. That is the new birth of water and of spirit.

Water symbolizes a certain idea of cleanliness, purification and preparation in the personality; and the spirit symbolizes the fire that illuminates the conscience in the higher reality of the great divine self.

In the Sermon on the Mount, the Master Jesus repeats many times: *"In truth, I say to you"*. This is to show that he is deriving his inspiration from the Sun of Truth, and, also, that the light of truth is passing through his own awakened self. He also means: *"Through me, it is the great 'I', the great 'I Am' that speaks to you."*

The great *"I Am"* is the source of all things, the universal Word that the Master St. John described in his gospel. Thus, the divine being can pass directly through the awakened self of any human who is correctly prepared.

This is the great revelation of Christ, and it is what the Rose+Cross has been, and is, working on in secret. It is the very principle of democracy, although the final outcome is much more elevated, much more sublime; it is the principle of a living community of free individualities.

Very few humans are able to understand these ideas in purity. Those who can are ready to enter, and to take part in the work of our sacred Brotherhood-Sisterhood of the Rose+Cross.

The Mystery of the Resurrection of the Dead

In the holy writings of all peoples, it is said that, one day, the dead will come out of their tombs and be resurrected; this is an allusion to the mysteries of the rebirth of the superior self within individuals. As long as man does not know his superior, divine nature, he is considered to be dead; and his body, his personality, represent his tomb and his shroud. Coming out of the tomb and being resurrected—that is precisely what it is to be initiated, to wake up to the light of the divine and primordial Self that lives buried in everyone coming into the world.

Materialistic Christians take these words literally, and expect to see the dead coming out of tombs; but this is an illusion. The truth is much more beautiful than all the lies.

Christ came to teach this path of the resurrection of man's superior self, which is the resurrection of the divine in humanity. But the world did not understand it; and that is why the closed, secret circle of the Johannite Christians has kept and cultivated this teaching.

The call to brotherhood-sisterhood that the Rose+Cross sent out in Europe in the 1600's *(Fama Fraternitatis)*, and which can still be heard today, is a call to resurrection, to initiation. If this call was correctly understood, it could be the starting point of a real revolution for humanity, the beginning of a new era; and we could then, once again, set the counter back to zero.

Of course, between the moment when one hears and understands the call within and the moment when they are truly resurrected, there is a period of preparation that can be more or less long. Most humans have heard the call of the light, but they did not take any notice of it, and it was forgotten. It happened during a moment of solitude, out in nature, or looking up at the stars in the sky, at the time of a great trial in life, or at the moment of a brush with death; a higher state of being—clear, peaceful, harmonious, cosmic—manifested itself, and then you understood the real meaning of your life. But then you were taken over again by the preoccupations of everyday life, of the limited and mortal self.

Everything in our society today is designed to increase the preoccupations of the mortal self. This is a very clear sign of a dying culture. Only the sun of the higher self can give an impulse of life to our society.

Those who are sufficiently prepared when they hear this call start down the path, searching, and can be led to meet us. That is when the preparation begins, to enable them to live more and more in the reality of the divine self.

When the individual meets the community of light, they are given a private lesson; this cannot be done without mutual cooperation, because it involves the communication of truth of a spiritual and invisible order.

Suffice it to say here that the Rose+Cross current, faithful to the impulse of Christ in the Master Jesus, works so that all of humanity may live this experience of the resurrection in authentic individuality, in the true being of man.

The Model of Man

When Pilate says, pointing at the Master Jesus, *"Here is the Man"*, he pronounces a mantra of absolutely immeasurable significance. This is telling us: "Here is the model of the man that everyone should be." It is for this reason that the enlightened Brothers and Sisters of the Rose+Cross have accorded great importance to the book *The Imitation of Jesus Christ*, and to the words of our beloved guide, Christian Rose+Cross: *"Jesus is everything to me."* These words have a very profound esoteric meaning.

It is clear that, if people lose the model of the good and just man, they become worse than animals, committing atrocities that are foreign to the realm of animals. Give humanity a bad upbringing, an erroneous education, and it can lose control, and breed monsters capable of the worst crimes, of violations against human rights and against the right to precious life. Do you understand now the great need for an education guided by the Rose+Cross—one which frees people from the slavery of the inferior nature and leads towards the good light of the soul, towards the knowledge of the true divine nature, with the worthy attitude of respect for life?

Without this enlightened training, people will never know the dignity and invulnerability attached to the quality of being a man. Besides, what do we know about man at the present time? We have dissected him to study his anatomy. We have gone a bit astray in psychology, and we are lost at sea with psychiatry.

But what about man as a living soul, as a cosmic being— eternal, divine? Here we know nothing; and yet this aspect is the most important one, if we really want to educate and guide humankind.

The Healing of Humanity

We are obliged to recognize that, two thousand years ago, Pilate knew more about what is essential in the human being than the greatest materialistic minds of our time.

When he said *"Here is the Man"*, he was talking about the invisible, divine aspect of the Master Jesus, and not his organs or his body.

If we, too, are successful in contemplating, in our own spirits, the spiritual body of the Master Jesus, we can conclude that contemporary humanity is profoundly sick. In fact, the one who is unconscious of the light of their superior nature, and who lives only in their inferior being, has to be sick. The one who finds fulfillment in crime, depravity, lies, and all kinds of illusions, is ill.

The very essence of man is goodness, along with all of the divine qualities and virtues.

That is why the Brothers and Sisters of the universal Brotherhood-Sisterhood are represented as therapists. This word "therapist" has been greatly misunderstood. In its most profound meaning, it is identical to Jesus—he who comes down from heaven to heal the suffering of the world.

So the Rose+Cross was not content just to preach the good word, but did something tangible, by starting to treat the great sickness of humanity; and this is why they were persecuted, because a certain intelligence in the world does not want man to wake up and be healed. They have already put Christ to death, so why should they stop? They put him to death in the name of God, in the name of good and of reason. But only lies come out of their mouths, because their gifts are war, illness, death, poverty, destruction.

This, however, is the intelligence that the world follows, and it is why the Rose+Cross works in silence for the healing of humanity.

This healing of illnesses by the Order of the Rose+Cross is, in reality, a great divine service which is carried out in silence and at no cost by each Brother and Sister of the Brotherhood-Sisterhood.

They practice a sacred medicine of which the world knows nothing.

The Great Reality of Man

The question is this: is one a man because of looking like one, or does being a man mean having developed within oneself certain human virtues and qualities? So, when you really love someone, is it only their organs that you appreciate, or is it the whole being, with their character, soul and mind?

If man was only what the materialistic scientists study, a mass of organs, then life would have no meaning. But the great reality of man is, above all, invisible; it is his soul. Therefore, one is not born a man; one becomes a man by developing certain virtues within oneself.

For us, that which never dies—that which was, is, and always will be—the eternal: that is man. Of course, one can then recognize that man also has a lower nature, resembling an animal, which can be domesticated, and can become extremely valuable and rich in hidden treasures. As long as man is unacquainted with the eternal part of himself, he has every chance of being reduced to slavery by his lower nature and of being led, in spite of himself, into committing crimes. These crimes are the result of a sickness which can be treated by using Christ's great remedy.

If you yourself are interested in the teaching of the Rose+Cross, be aware of the blessing of being born in human form because this opens up great possibilities to accomplish good for all beings. If you wish to, you can live in love, wisdom and truth. On earth, only the awakened human being can be aware of this choice and can, fully consciously, experience it in life.

Today, people think that everything is owed to them, but this type of mentality can only make them poor. Those who are intelligent rejoice in the fact that they have a human body and try to be worthy of it. Therefore, they respect all people and, also, all the inferior beings, which are aspiring to become human also.

The Faithful Guardians of the Divine Mysteries

Now, some seekers who are widely read might be surprised that we associate the very holy and enlightened Brotherhood-Sisterhood of the Rose+Cross with the solar being of Christ, because they think that the Brotherhood-Sisterhood descends from certain Egyptian mysteries. In reality, the Rose+Cross has always existed, from the very beginning of the spiritual history of humanity, and it has always served the being of Christ.

Christ himself existed long before his incarnation in the Master Jesus. At the moment when humanity fell into materialism, the Order of the Rose+Cross was created as the faithful guardian of the divine mysteries and the spiritual guide for developing humanity.

The first man was conceived in the divine image and the result of the Fall was the loss of this divine image. Human beings, progressing through the material world, are searching for their true identity. The Order of the Rose+Cross was asked to keep safe the image of the original man: Christ. This man bears no resemblance to man as known on earth. This is the cosmic man, who fills the whole, visible and invisible, universe.

Thus, the Rose+Cross, faithful to its original mission, has worked relentlessly to prepare humanity for the divine and liberating revelation of which it is the guardian. Egypt, like the work of the Master Jesus, was only a step toward the achievement of its mission.

An ancient cabalistic legend contains the profound secrets which we are touching lightly upon here; it says that an angel named Raziel had bequeathed to Adam, the original man, a book containing all the secrets of creation, but that this book was taken away after the Fall.

What the initiatic legend does not say is that the angel Raziel, or Roziel, who lives in the sephiroth Chokmah, the region of the cosmic Word, of Christ, in the cabalistic Tree of Life, gathered around itself a circle of disciples—the Rose+Cross—and gave them the book of divine secrets. This angel is, and remains, the protector and the inspiring force of the Brothers and Sisters of the Rose+Cross, the faithful guardians of the divine mysteries. This sublime angel has always served Christ, and has worked with him, over the centuries, to reveal the true image of light of the original man. Only this image, properly understood, has the power to free humanity from the evil which dominates it.

The New Can Only Be Created by the Youngest

When Christ, embodied in the Master Jesus, said: *"I did not come to abolish the ancient prophets, but to accomplish their words"*, he was clearly revealing the work of the universal Brotherhood-Sisterhood, and, also, that a step had been taken in the history of humanity.

So those who do not include the great reality of Christ and the work of Christian Rose+Cross in the history of our

Brotherhood-Sisterhood are behind the times, and are drawing their water from erroneous sources. It is necessary to have the courage to admit it without any prejudice. Because there is a rumor which implies that the great individuality of Christian Rose+Cross is a myth; so, in that case, why would not Christ himself be a myth, as many people would like to make us believe? These people will surely succeed in doing so one day, if the cosmic intelligence gives them enough time.

Reasoning like this only proves the ignorance about real spiritual and initiatic processes. One can love the Rose+Cross from the outside, and wish to form an assembly of people in its name; but that is a phenomenon which originates from human will and not from the great reality of the spirit.

Such a process, where everything is based on tradition, on the past, generates nothing new. This can be summarized in these words: "Once upon a time, in Egypt, the universal Brotherhood-Sisterhood manifested itself and made the source of the spirit flow; and now, we want to re-light that flame."

But, in reality, humanity evolves, and what manifests itself in the present is the most important.

The new can only be created by the youngest, the one who is eternally young precisely because that youngest one possesses the power to rejuvenate life.

The Great Inspiration and Guide of the Modern Rose+Cross

This youngest one was designated by Christ in the individuality of the Master St. John, the beloved disciple.

St. John the Baptist symbolized the end of an ancient world, and St. John the Evangelist the beginning of a new one.

The Master St. John has not stopped incarnating to fulfill his mission of preparing for the coming of the Solar Culture. It is he who, having taken the name of Christian Rose+Cross, renewed the Order. Every hundred years, he is incarnated on earth to revitalize his disciples. So his influence has never stopped growing in an invisible way, and his disciples can communicate with him through mysteries which only they understand.

The Master St. John, alias Christian Rose+Cross, is the only great Master, guide and inspiration of the noble gathering of the Brothers and Sisters of the contemporary Rose+Cross.

Without his magical presence, no assembly can truly work under the symbol of the Rose+Cross because nothing new comes to illuminate the work.

Tradition and Present Reality

So tradition is not everything, and the living experience of the reality in the present moment is also one of the pillars of the temple of mysteries. The union of the two pillars is necessary for the equilibrium of the building. For example, many people were interested in the Pharaoh Ischnaton or Akhnaton because he belonged to the universal Brotherhood-Sisterhood in Egypt at the time of the Pharaohs. They drew spiritual conclusions from his teaching; that is the tradition. But Omraam Michael Aivanhov, who conducted initiatic teaching in France, was actually the reincarnation of the being who was formerly Ischnaton; and those people who are so passionate about the past did not see the new, the youngest, the one who actually brings life, and is right here in the present moment in a real way.

What they were studying with so much passion was, in reality, ancient and dead. Only a true student of the Rose+Cross can understand this.

We must have a great respect for tradition but we must also want to turn towards the youngest who arises in the present moment to rejuvenate life. It is only this youngest one who has the power to realize the sacred teaching. By turning away from him, to live in the comfort of the past, we are distancing ourselves from the real initiation. It is so nice to venerate a Master or a teaching that is no longer alive because we are not required to change, to make any effort, to question ourselves within what is real.

Therefore, those who do not include the hidden

Christianity, and especially those who say that Christian Rose+Cross is a myth, separate themselves from the youngest, from the great work accomplished without respite by the Master St. John in the bosom of the Order of the Rose+Cross.

The kingdom of God, the celestial Jerusalem, cannot come from below; humans cannot generate it by themselves, even with the strongest will and the good intentions of which some are capable.

The kingdom of light must come from the heavens, from the great reality of the omnipresent spirit in the youngest.

The Exercise of the Dew and the Crucible

That is why a disciple trains himself consciously to welcome, every day at dawn, the youngest, the sacred impulse which rejuvenates life and carries it forward.

Doing this exercise is the equivalent of collecting the morning dew fallen from the sky. This is why some people have explained that the expression Rose+Cross signifies the dew and the crucible to collect it in. The crucible represents the path of tradition, and the dew is the youngest, the mystery of the life-giving spirit.

The crucible is also the human body: the cross; and the dew is the divine spirit which comes down from heaven to enlighten it.

The dew also symbolizes water, and the cross the structure of light of the universe, the living fire.

Explaining these mysteries would take us too far, but let's simply say that we find in them the forces which generate the second birth, the rebirth and the resurrection of water and of fire, which we have already touched upon.

This symbol of the crucible and the dew teaches us that the awakened man is able to use his body (the crucible) to receive very high spiritual influences (the dew), in order to introduce them into life on earth and to use them to perform wonderful work.

It is in order to make this work possible that the Rose+Cross teaches its students the laws of the regeneration of the body, and of its rejuvenation (1). This has never been clearly understood by the world, and has given birth to a whole series of legends. The world, refusing to elevate itself, wants to drag down to its own vibratory level everything that it does not understand.

---

(1) Consult the teachings-by-correspondence of the School of Life and Spirit founded by Olivier Manitara. (Editor's note).

The Exercise for Contacting the Brotherhood-Sisterhood of Light

Try to experience the fact that your physical body is alive and think about how you can keep it healthy and best prepare it to become a receiver and a transmitter of the noblest and purest spiritual vibrations and rays. In this way, you could become, more and more, a healer of the soul of the world in the bosom of our noble assembly of light.

When your physical body is prepared in this way, train yourself to keep it under your control and perfectly immobile. In this position, find within yourself the inner attitude of calm, and of the presence of the spirit.

Next, become aware of the exterior space which surrounds you. Consciously think of the words of the Rose+Cross: *"There is no empty space."*

You can then arrive at the point of living this experience, in which you become aware that the air is full of spirit and life, and that it contains Everything possible.

For example, if you decide to think "light", light comes into this space with a whole magnetic field, a soul which is tied to it.

If you think "darkness", the same phenomenon occurs, accompanied by another ambiance.

And if, in this way, you think of the Master St. John, of Christian Rose+Cross and, through him, of Christ in man, you can—if you are worthy and capable of it—be accepted into the very venerable Brotherhood-Sisterhood and take your first steps on the path of service to humanity. But, for that, you must be ready, because your steps must not be guided by vain curiosity, by vanity or by snobbishness. Be aware that here we are touching upon the greatest and most sacred mysteries of humanity, and that the holy guides must not be disturbed by things that do not concern them. Only authentic love and the noble aspiration to serve the divine can motivate contact with the Brotherhood-Sisterhood of light. This contact can, in addition, be obtained in a concrete fashion through the School of Life and Spirit, which conveys, in a new way, the initiatic teaching of the stream of humanity of St. John and of the Cosmic Tradition.

To accomplish exercises like these in complete safety, it is preferable to be under the protection and blessing of the field of life of this type of free, spiritual School of life and spirit.

The Aura and the Will of Christian Rose+Cross

If you correctly perform the exercise which we have just revealed, you will be able to perceive for yourself why we focus on the individuality of Christian Rose+Cross, of the Master St. John.

79

He is the true guide of all Rosicrucians, and the inspiration for all the initiates and Masters of our present cycle. Of course, there are other Masters of the Cosmic Tradition; but, in the spiritual world, it is a law that all real Masters, whatever their degree of elevation, must put themselves behind the king of the era, to support him in his actions and his mission.

This Master, full of love and compassion, works hard for the triumph of the great liberty and creativity of humanity. Such liberty flows automatically from an enlightenment and an elevation of all individuals, freely chosen and fully conscious.

All true Rosicrucians live in the aura and the will of Christian Rose+Cross, of the Christian with the Rose and the Cross, who acts in the contemporary world equally as well in the visible and the invisible.

This individuality-guide is absolutely not mythical, but works relentlessly for the safekeeping of the true, western and world, mysteries. The world would truly be surprised if it could consult the secret archives of our Order, to see all the things in our modern society that had their origins in the Rose+Cross.

All this justifies Christ's words about his beloved disciple: *"I want him to stay until I come."*

Christ is the highest divine manifestation that has occurred on earth through a human being. Its aim is to elevate the consciousness and life of all humans to the same level as that which the Master Jesus was able to live. That is what he calls his future coming, and, for that, he clearly designates the Master St. John as the bearer of this mission. To accomplish it, the Master will reincarnate every hundred years, which is a huge sacrifice on his part. He will always reincarnate with his disciples, who will progressively increase in number to help him in his saintly mission.

Christians should meditate on the words of their Master and savior, but conditions on earth today are so difficult that we often forget the true goal of our incarnation.

There is nothing more sublime than to serve Christ, enlightened humanity, infinite love. That is the true goal of incarnation and life on earth.

May those who have ears to hear and eyes to see use them to understand the words of the spirit.

Only He Who Resembles Christ Can Understand Christianity

One of the great works of the enlightened Brothers and Sisters was to unite, within their working circle, all of the influences, religions and cultures of all peoples with the mysteries of Christianity, in order to renew and rejuvenate them. That is why the Rose+Cross became the keeper of the sacred stream of

Cosmic Tradition. In this way, all of the spiritual life of humanity was unified and harmonized within the mutual respect.

Rose+Cross members carry in their souls the inner vision of the greatness of Christ, who is the living source which gave birth to all of the spiritual currents of different peoples and cultures. Reuniting culture in the present with its original source of creation is to heal and rejuvenate it.

The Rosicrucian movement, whose inspiration is truly Christian in the unknown sense of the word, has, however, been persecuted, throughout its different manifestations, as an anti-Christian society. This shows us, once again, the illusion of the world. People think they know what Christianity is, they think they understand Christ, even though it is clear that only those who have made themselves resemble Christ can understand him.

When we speak of Christianity, people shrug their shoulders, because everyone thinks they already know what it is; and you, dear reader, you surely think so, too.

Well, this is the kind of dead idea that closes the doors to the true knowledge that gives new life. The ones who think they know remain closed to the discovery of the hidden spirit that animates things and beings. We assert that Christianity has not yet come into the world; in order for it to come, human beings must become the man John, the beloved disciple. This is a state of being, which, when achieved, makes it possible for human beings to receive Christ, and opens up one's powers of comprehension to the most hidden mysteries.

Being a real disciple of Christ is possessing an inner light; but, before that, it is better to admit humbly that we know nothing about Christianity. That leaves the door open and allows every possibility to show itself.

How could one be a disciple of Christ without ever having met him? It is just a label that one sticks to one's clothing, but there is no authenticity in it. One then gives oneself permission, in the name of Christ, to judge and even to kill others, like the catholic bishops in the martyred town of Beziers in France, who, when asked by their mercenaries how they could distinguish the Cathars from the Christians during the planned massacre of that city, answered: "Kill them all; God will recognize his own."

However, Christ had said: *"You will recognize my disciples in those who have love."* The Cathars, our beloved Brothers and Sisters, were the true disciples of Christ, of the good and worthy man, and lived out his words: *"You will be killed because of my name."*

The Experience of Giving Yourself Totally

The one who truly wishes to enter into living initiatic knowledge is under an obligation to set aside certain hypothetical ideas and beliefs of the personality, to open themselves up, in a new way, to the life which is coming now. It is necessary to cast off the ancient, dead conception of Christianity, to open up to the truth, the one that touches the deepest part of the being—awakening the soul to freedom, to the great reality of the treasure of inner light.

Only they who are walking the path of the Cross; who have given up all of their false inner conceptions; who have known the suffering and the solitude of the world; who have, at last, been crucified in their lower nature and known the rebirth of the spirit—only they can truly understand something of the Christianity of the Rose+Cross.

They will understand, within themselves, Christ's grandeur and importance for humanity, as no word can describe it.

True Christianity requires the total crucifixion of the lower nature, the gift without restriction, the total transformation. Christ is a global being, and it is unhealthy to fragment him, to divide him up. Some people, having met him, choose only the humanitarian aspect, but leave the rest aside. They keep within themselves a place reserved for the lower nature, and then are surprised when the light starts to fade away and leave them.

When the disciple stands before the light of the superior self of humanity, his being must be completely open and receptive;

otherwise, he cannot receive the teaching in the right way.

Nowadays humans are filled to overflowing with all sorts of information and useless facts; there is no longer any room for the inner light of the soul.

The Master Jesus did not give only half of himself; he gave the absolute gift of his being, because he knew that divine teaching is a whole, and that a part which is separated from the Whole starts inevitably to waste away.

The Brotherhood-Sisterhood teaches in a clear and living way that the true knowledge of Christ is the most important, the most essential, for it leads to fullness. In this, it is in perfect harmony with these mantric words: *"First look for the kingdom of heaven and its justice, and all the rest will be given to you in addition."*

So, instead of just one part, welcome all of the light; offer your whole chalice to receive it. Then you will be protected against the impurities and the mistakes of the world.

When you take a shower, you do not wash only the visible parts of your body (hands and face), but your whole body, to stay in good health.

Those who aspire to experience Christ must do so totally, and not just halfway. If they find later that this experience is not good for them, they can always go back to their old life; they are still free.

There are those who only choose small pieces, fragments of

Christ's teachings, by, for example, going to church to hear a sermon, giving to the poor, taking part in humanitarian works, etc.—in order to have a clear conscience. They call themselves Christians, but they divide Christ and belittle him; and, therefore, they can not really get close to him. It is better to remain humble and modest before the light, rather than to reduce it by one's fear of looking at it as it is, in all its splendor.

Christ is unity and the unification of multiple voices. Man must bow down before him, and his lower nature must be totally sacrificed and transformed in the crucible. That is when the Rose will bloom—the Rose of the divine nature that man was already carrying within without knowing it.

Fortunately, the true universal Christianity, that of the Cosmic Tradition, could not be weakened, because it remained pure and intact in its unity and universality, through the Johannite current of the Rose+Cross.

In the light of Christian Rose+Cross, greetings and peace.

Solis Deo Gloria

Living one's true nature,
consciously experiencing divine unity
and embodying it through the personality—
that is the highest initiation.

The Circle of Light of the Cosmic Tradition

The Magical Work of the Inner Community

In every time period and in every domain, there have been beings who have advanced humanity by their discoveries, their teachings, their living example. These beings were, consciously or unconsciously, in contact with the spiritual world, and they were merely manifesting to the outside world what they saw there, so that it, too, could participate and advance.

If we take the case of the great spiritual teachers and legislators—like Zoroaster, Buddha, or the Master Jesus—we see that a group of close disciples, a holy circle of light, always forms around them. We find this magical circle of the inner community in all the peoples and spiritual cultures throughout human history. They are the twelve disciples gathered around Christ, the twelve knights of the Round Table, the twelve Brothers of the initiatic council of the Order of the Temple, and also the twelve Masters assembled around Christian Rose+Cross during the secret incarnation of the idealistic and mystical Brotherhood-Sisterhood in Europe.

The individuality of Christian Rose+Cross called around itself twelve Masters with whom it worked, in the utmost secrecy, during several incarnations, to establish this school of the Cosmic Tradition on earth, and to prepare for the coming of Christ into a great number of minds in a correct and liberating way.

This circle of light opened up progressively and began to radiate into the world. What was radiating was the etheric body of Christian Rose+Cross, which had fused with Christ. This fusion did not operate in the same way as with the Master Jesus because St. John developed within himself the impulse of Christ brought through the Master Jesus. So what happened in the mysteries of Palestine was a purely divine intervention which came to transform humanity in the person of the Master Jesus. This impulse then belonged to every human. It was up to them to cultivate this seed planted in their interior soil. The Master St. John was the first to do this; he developed the seed of Christ within himself and lived it, as every man can and must do. Once the seed was developed, he radiated it through a circle of twelve Masters of the ancient mysteries, and that is how the young Rosicrucian school was born, for a new manifestation in the heart of Europe. Each of the twelve took several students, until the Master St. John reincarnated and appeared under the name of Christian Rose+Cross to work with his new disciples. One hundred years later, the Brotherhood-Sisterhood sent its call out into the world. Since then, the Brothers and Sisters, gentle and humble of heart, have worked relentlessly for the harmonious and healthy development of humanity and the earth.

The Etheric Body of Christian Rose+Cross

Each time a new student enters the Brotherhood-Sisterhood, the etheric body of Christian Rose+Cross becomes stronger. This etheric body contains the indispensable atmosphere that enables the seed of Christ placed in every man to grow and flourish in the best conditions.

This seed cannot develop in the atmosphere of the world; only the etheric body of Christian Rose+Cross can provide it with the food and the vibration that it needs.

This etheric body of Christ does not act only through Christian Rose+Cross, but also, and in the same way, through all of his authentic disciples, through every Rose+Cross. The individuality of Christian Rose+Cross is incarnated every hundred years, to renew and, above all, to keep pure, this etheric body. This is the reason why it is said that "he always incarnates in the same body", because it is the etheric body of the Order. These are very sacred mysteries.

In our time, this etheric body must be amplified again so that it touches not only the members inside the Order, but also a great number of people in the outside world.

This is a real inner call which must be sent out in the direction of humanity. To enter the etheric body of the Rose+Cross is to perceive and recognize, in a free way, the body of the living Christ on earth and in oneself, in one's soul.

The Living Word of a Master

If all the great teachers of humanity have established around themselves a circle of light, it is simply to seal an alliance with the cosmic hierarchy and the celestial order.

Through such an available and suitably prepared circle, through such a cup of the Holy Grail, that which is not of the world can penetrate into the world. This is the great secret, stated in a simple way. It is the secret of the community of the well-intentioned. When a being like Christ manifests himself on earth, humanity cannot understand his words, for they are too sublime.

When he says: *"God is love"*, we think we understand; but, in reality, these words are, first and foremost, spirit and life, and that is what is most important. And, even if we really analyze the situation, we perceive very quickly that not everyone is likely to grasp the real, living, profound meaning of such a statement coming out of the mouth of a spiritual Master.

The teaching of a guide of humanity is always transmitted in the present for evolution in the future. The man who receives a seed cannot know that it will later grow into a huge tree. He will become aware of that in the future.

Therefore, the teaching is not given to everyone, but only to those who are likely to receive it in the right way. These are the disciples, the men and women awakened to the force of limitless good, who aspire to understand the mysteries of life and to serve the beautiful, the just and the true in humanity, beyond every obstacle.

The work of a disciple is to receive within the words of wisdom of the Universal Teaching, to give them life in the soul, and to practice them in life. It is by the intermediary of the circle of light of the conscientious and honest disciples that the word of the authentic Master can radiate throughout the earth and touch humanity.

We can hear the words *"God is love"* and find them very

beautiful. You can even repeat them yourself. However, in reality, they sound very different when they are spoken by an ordinary being, instead of by Christ himself. It is precisely this difference that one must feel absolutely; that is where the path of initiation begins.

What is important is not the dead word but the living word, which only Christ can pronounce. It is this living word that the disciples of the inner community are required to receive and cultivate.

If this word is not consciously cultivated, it can fade away and disappear like the seeds, in the gospel parable, that fell on infertile ground.

There Is a Difference Between Hearing and Understanding

Many sincere seekers aspire to knowledge but, when they find themselves in front of an authentic spiritual guide, the liberating teaching cannot be communicated to them. It is not that the guide does not want to—quite the contrary. It is, rather, that such communication is very difficult to realize; it demands a whole process, a complete preparation.

To tell a being that *"God is love"* is not enough; the idea of God must already be awakened within so that the soul can be ignited by these living words spoken by a Master of light, who lives them within, in purity.

The role of an inner spiritual community is to be specially trained to receive a system of special knowledge in a correct way, to cultivate it, to spread it, and to realize it.

The Brotherhood-Sisterhood of the Rose+Cross represents this kind of living community, which has, since the beginning of time, received the sacred deposit of the Cosmic Tradition and of the teaching of Christ: the original man.

All of the humans around the world who make themselves receptive to this inner light are immediately contacted by the Brotherhood-Sisterhood. Nothing—not distance, not time, not isolation—can prevent the reception of the teaching, of the vibration of our divine school.

The one who is not ready can hear the teaching externally, but there is a great difference between hearing and understanding. Understanding is a spiritual phenomenon which happens in the soul. The process of understanding means that one has elevated oneself to the same vibratory level as the source of the teaching. So, truly to understand Christ is to be a part of his life, and, therefore, of the etheric body of our beloved guide, Christian Rose+Cross.

The goal of an outer initiatic school is to lead the pilgrims on the path to a gradual understanding of the universal inner teaching. There are different degrees of understanding, and those who think they understand before they have reached the summit are mistaken; on the other hand, those who are aware that they have not yet reached the summit and that they do not yet have a global understanding are on the path to initiation. Knowing that you do not know everything, and remaining open and respectful, while working to improve yourself, is a good attitude for a healthy life.

The Rose+Cross Is the Mediator Between Christ and Humanity

Knowing that one does not know is the beginning of true understanding, which is inexpressible. Real knowledge is only produced by a fusion, a union, a free osmosis, from soul to soul. This is the meaning of the community of light, the meaning of a spiritual communion around a divine principle. The Rose+Cross is such a community around the principle of Christ, of the original man. The body of Christian Rose+Cross is the mediator between Christ and humanity. It is required to go on working until Christ comes into humanity once again. It is through his intermediary that he will manifest himself; that is quite logical. Someone who makes a great discovery in nuclear physics gathers together a group of physicists to convey it to the world. Only such a group is able to understand it; and if there is no such group, then the discoverer is obliged to create one, and the discovery cannot be transmitted because everything has to be started all over again from the beginning.

Within such a group of physicists, there circulates a school of thought, which grows over the centuries and becomes capable of inspiring the knowledge of physics by itself. These are immutable laws.

The Necessity for the Inner Group of the Mysteries of Christ

If one studies the case of the Master Jesus, one notices that, often, the people wanted to stone him because they did not understand his teaching. That is when one can grasp the usefulness of the inner current, which reacts in a positive way. The teaching of Christ was too strong for the people, too revolutionary and initiatic. It was fundamental for the future of humanity that this teaching be received correctly, and with the right understanding—the one that generates new life. It was also crucial that the inner community should survive in purity and continue on through the centuries, because the outer group formed by Christ became dogmatic and was the first to persecute the living inner teaching. So, if the spirit of Christ showed itself again today, the Christian church would undoubtedly be the last to recognize it. Christ would upset too many established concepts, and would speak about far too many unknown and new things. But, in reality, the impulse of Christ has not left the earth; it radiates through his secret and living school—St. John's stream of humanity.

When Christ asks his disciples to keep themselves ready because he will come in a sudden and unexpected way, he is speaking to the inner group and reminding it of the necessity for preparation and vigilance.

At the moment when Christ shows himself, the community must be able to recognize him immediately and to serve him. This is why the school of St. John has remained very secret in its nucleus. Each time a member disappeared, they left behind several disciples, one of which was secretly chosen to succeed. That one would then receive intensive training. The world has never known anything about these impenetrable mysteries; it has only been able to see their external manifestations. Reaching back to the source of these mysteries is equivalent to meeting Christ and his enlightened humanity; and this is something that the world does not want.

We can experience in our souls a feeling of gratitude and love for these servants of Good who work in the shadows, looking after the teaching of the true and pure man. Never will the world, with its current mentality, be able to penetrate the mysteries of this central nucleus of the teaching of Christ.

A Brother or Sister chosen to work in this secret nucleus will never be able to be part of it again. In their future incarnations, they will have to put themselves at the service of the outer Order as a priest, artist, healer and teacher in the highest, the most noble, and the solar sense of the word.

A Brother's or Sister's only homeland is the world of light and they are aware that, on earth, they are only a transient, a walker, a pilgrim! Therefore, they do not belong to any particular group of people; they belong, above all, to themselves and to the Heavenly Father.

A real Rose+Cross is free and allows others to be free, never subjecting anyone to their will or imposing their knowledge.

Their life is an example, and, through it, they teach and heal. When humans decide to help that Brother or Sister, they do it on their own, by their own inner spirit, because they have recognized in them the solar force of Good at work in the cosmos, and in everything that lives.

Such a Brother or Sister has a much greater radiance than the central nucleus, and, so, through them, the light can penetrate more deeply into humanity, in all the areas of life, to help and guide for the better. This is why many schools and organizations have claimed to be tied to the Rose+Cross.

The Society of the Invisible

It is not without reason that the saintly and noble Brotherhood-Sisterhood has also been called the society of the invisible. We have already said that one of the goals of the Order is to promote a true knowledge of the human being, and, especially, of the fact that what is essential in man is, precisely, invisible. The real man is invisible, and this is true for you, as well. What is the most important in you is what cannot be seen. The physical body reveals a part of the invisible man while, at the same time, hiding a larger part.

This is one of the great concepts of the Rose+Cross, and, if you become aware of it, you can be transformed and achieve a great step forward in your evolution.

Now, if the essential in man is invisible, this is also true for everything that surrounds us, and, notably, for history. True history is invisible and, therefore, secret. Very few people have a correct idea of true history and are able to go back to the source of the causes which triggered certain "historical" events. To truly understand an act, one must include the invisible thinking that motivated it. Materialistic historians take into account only the external view of things, and are interested only in the dead aspect. They have invented a false history, and humanity has not been able to draw the right conclusions about certain unfortunate events.

And it can also be said that even true life is invisible and that it is in this domain that we must go looking for it.

When we say that somebody has "something in the back of their mind", we are alluding to the invisible phenomenon which directs their life and their actions. Now we need to be able to know exactly what this idea is, where it comes from, what it means, and in which direction it will lead man. Until humanity has mastered this process, it will be impossible consciously to participate in the secret web of the history of the world, which is the history of the divine plan for humanity and its planet of life, as well as the history of the *"combat of the children of light against the sons of darkness"*, as described in the Essene manuscripts of the Dead Sea.

The Mental Manipulation of Humanity

It is so easy to manipulate a being who does not know that true life is invisible and who, therefore, trusts only in appearances—which, as everybody knows, are deceiving.

Many beings say they fight against manipulators, but they are the first to manipulate the crowds: "they have something in the back of their minds." The only way to avoid manipulators is to reveal to humans their true nature as invisible and divine beings.

There is no other way.

Now, how many people have venerated beings like Hitler, giving them all their confidence; and how many became his militant followers, believing they were doing the right thing, provoking and directing hatred against a category of people? It is easy to say now that we are against Hitler, but maybe we are still voting for him by participating in the system of criticism and hate being developed today by the media and certain groups. We do all this without thinking; but, in the end, are we moving towards Christ, the good and strong man, or towards the enraged and destructive beast?

It is an immutable law that humans—by their thoughts, their feelings and their actions—draw to themselves a leader. May they unite with us, the Brothers and Sisters of the Rose+Cross, to call upon the good, humble and gentle-hearted man!

"You who labor under a heavy burden, come to me, the I-Am, and I will comfort you.

Take up my yoke and put yourself in my school because I am gentle and humble of heart, and you will find comfort for your soul.

My yoke is easy and my burden light."

We need you; you are indispensable for the positive progress of humanity. You, too, can be part of history and help enlightened humanity to bring about the triumph of love, of wisdom, and of the great truth. So hear the call and join us.

The Energy of Success and the Presence of the Saintly Assembly

In the call sent out in France by the Brotherhood-Sisterhood in the 16th century, we can see clearly pointed out the importance of the conscious thought of the invisible aspect of man and of nature:

"We, delegates of the Brethren of the Rose+Cross, are visiting, in both a visible and an invisible manner, this town, by the grace of the All-High, towards whom turn the hearts of the wise. We learn, without any kind of external means, to speak the language of the country where we are living, and we pull men, our fellow creatures, out of the clutches of terror and death.

If someone wishes to see us only out of curiosity, he will never communicate with us; but if he sincerely wishes to be registered as a member of our Brotherhood, we, who judge thoughts, will show him the truth of our promises, so much so that we give no indication of the place where we reside, because thought, fused with the real will of the reader, will be able to make each of us known to the other."

It is only after a long period of aimless wandering that man understands the meaning of the call, and that, above all, there where resides the community of the wise whose hearts are turned towards the All-High, there also resides the energy of success, of the victory of light.

When man is not within the energy of success, it is because, somewhere, he is tied to the community of traitors, of those who betray the divine image of the true man. The one who takes away from man his high ideal of perfection cuts him off from the help of the holy gathering and plunges him into darkness. However, the holy gathering is always present in and around you, and you can, at any moment, call upon it to ask it for help and assistance. This depends only on your thought and your will.

The Rosicrucian Teaching

If joy lights up within you at the thought of the Rose+Cross, you are ready to know its mysteries.

Our alliance of light is filled with joy and gratitude. That is what carries us on the wings of divine service, and so the work comes easily to us.

The Rose+Cross shows itself and spreads its teaching silently, through a smile, a friendly gesture, a helping hand in difficult times; a sign of comprehension, of compassion, of acceptance of another; by opening the prison gates, by healing and rejuvenating the sick, by breaking the chains of slavery of an old world; through the spontaneity of the new-born and the words of wisdom of the old; in the sparkling rays of the sun and the moon, of the stars and the oceans, of beauty and art.

The Rosicrucian teaching spreads silently through everything that is truly human, natural and divine.

We proclaim the triumph of light, the joy flowing through the holy community of the well-intentioned, the comprehension of life and the beauty of acting in cosmic unison.

He who stands before the gates of our School of life with the right attitude will not find the gates locked. It is people who lock themselves out of the land of success and happiness, by criticizing and refusing the great possibility of universal Good which is offered at every moment.

Everyone can have access to the teaching by showing his good faith, his love and his noble aspirations, through everyday actions.

If somebody accepts the statutes of our union of light, he will be accepted. Our statutes are clearly exposed in the world; just read the gospels and all the holy books of humanity with a new eye.

Fear Must Be Controlled

They who are afraid of losing their liberty by joining our alliance in the earthly reality are only showing by this that they are not yet free, because how can you lose something that you carry within your soul? Only those who really understand, and even revere, the liberty of the individual are ready to enter our Brotherhood-Sisterhood of good.

When fear controls the life of a man, it deprives him of his highest level of achievement. There is a great difference between discernment, prudence and fear. The first two qualities can be enlivened and put to good use by the conscious self. But fear comes from a negative atavism which submerges the self, diminishing it. So the man is directed by a force over which he has absolutely no control. The energy of fear must be controlled; that is certain.

The Sacred Current of Christ's Living Knowledge

The current of St. John and, within it, the Order of the Rose+Cross furnish all of the methods and exercises, the magnetic field and the guidance for perfection and ennoblement, so why deprive oneself of such help?

The seeker thinks he can find a little help only in books, or in external helps; but all of that is dead and, therefore, useless. Initiatic teaching is alive and lives in living beings. So it is to them that you must go; it is them that you must join, if you have heard the call.

Those who feel enlightened by reading the gospels are simply reading their own inner gospel. In this way, a book reveals the hidden life within you. You are the one who can open it or close it. If you have a profound perception, the gospel will speak to your soul; if you are superficial, you will see in it nothing more than a beautiful story.

The profound meaning of the gospels simply revealed your own ability to grasp the deep meaning of things. This is why we say that individuals themselves are the real instrument of knowledge, and that, by being immersed in the stream of life of St. John, they have every chance for harmonious development.

Living knowledge can only be held by living beings who experience it from the inside.

A book can describe what a tree is, but nothing can replace the real contact with a tree to obtain this knowledge.

In the school of St. John, the living knowledge of Christ has been passed from one living being to another for centuries, without any interruption. This process is in no way mechanical; it is a living, subtle and invisible process. It is a sort of spiritual transmission from soul to soul. One soul pours into another soul the spiritual contents of the etheric body of

Christian Rose+Cross and of the circle of the Masters of the Cosmic Tradition. This does not always happen through words; physical exercise and the sense of effort play a very important role. (1)

Keeping the Keys of Heaven and Earth

The school of St. John has many keys which open up the path to the spiritual, divine world, and to the true man. So that they will not be lost, these keys must not only be passed on, but also, above all, brought to life. Many of the keys possessed by the ancient wise have been lost, because they were not brought to life by a living group. Carrying such keys within oneself and working to keep them pure can be considered as a truly humanitarian service. Because man cannot find these keys by himself; they must absolutely be given from on high, through the incarnation of a celestial messenger.

For example, if the outer Christians lost a key given by Christ, they could never find it again because there is no messenger in their community and they waste no time pushing away the ones that come to visit them. In contrast, the school

(1) The School of Life and Spirit utilizes such living methods. (Editor's note).

of St. John and the Brotherhood-Sisterhood of the Rose+Cross are perpetually given life by their guide; this is what makes them strong. Christ said on this subject: *"I am with you until the end of time."*

These words are clear; but one must understand that, even during his incarnation, Christ was closer to St. John than to any other human. For this reason, we have to become like the man-John, like the disciple of Good, if we want to approach the beloved one of the human soul. This is a state of being which already lives within us and which we must attain.

When we speak about the vibration of the man-John, you must not think that you have to go back two thousand years. Since the mysteries of Palestine, man has changed; and this is why the ancient keys must be adapted to modern people.

When Christ gave him the keys of heaven and earth, St. Peter was deeply touched, and did everything to keep these keys in the best condition. St. Peter symbolizes the external church, and St. John the internal. Christ did not give St. John any keys, because he knew that man, the lock, was going to change and that St. John would, therefore, incessantly have to find new keys to bring his disciples towards Christ's state of being. What is important for the church of St. John is to reach Christ in the reality of life; and, for the church of St. Peter, it is to keep the keys, which hardly work anymore.

Christ taught St. John how to create keys that work in every lock, in every era. When the Brothers and Sisters of the Rose+Cross say that they learn to speak the language of the country in which they are living, they are talking about this mystery. Learning to speak the language of the country means knowing how to adapt the teaching to a given era and situation. It also means being in permanent union with the cosmic intelligence in order to know what it wants in each time period, and to act in harmony with it.

Thus, it is the enlightened intelligence of man which acts, according to the reality of the present life, and not through a rigid, outdated dogma.

A key which no longer works because the lock has changed is worthless; but the exoteric tradition always blames the lock for having evolved and continues to venerate the worthless key because it was given to them by their master a very long time ago. But the key is not important in itself; it has no value until the moment when it opens the gates of the kingdom of the good life, of absolute success. The key was made to be useful to man, and man should not be venerating the key. Such veneration is worthless, for the key is not a goal in itself.

The church of St. John was persecuted over the centuries because of this story of keys; and many men and women died horrible deaths because of these keys—and that continues to happen, even today. Humanity scrambles about after unimportant things, because it does not have a clear vision of the goal to be reached.

When Moses, Orpheus, Jesus or Mohammed gave the keys, it was to open the gates and enter into the light, and not to conserve them religiously, and kill for them.

A key is completely worthless if it is no longer capable of opening the door. But some people seized these keys to gain power over their brothers and sisters. They said: "I am the one who has the key; and, therefore, you must obey me blindly, you must worship the key." Do they really have the key to the land of the good life, they who do not enter there themselves? Christ said about these people: *"Woe to you who have the keys, and not only did not enter, but prevented others from entering."*

Some, seeing this, said: "The key is worthless, it is a fake; it is not a key because there is no door to open, and therefore no kingdom of light, no superior state of consciousness within man." But this reasoning is false because "where there is smoke, there is fire".

The Three Groups In Humanity

Therefore, there are three groups:

The group of the external circle, which looks after and worships the key that no longer opens anything;

The circle of those who have understood that the key does not work, and who think, therefore, that the door never existed;

And, lastly, the group of the inner circle, which is interested in the goal, and which has the means to open the door.

The first group thinks that the inner circle is heretical because it takes the liberty of transforming the teaching of the Master. It often considers itself to be superior, as the guardian of the real key.

The second group thinks that the inner circle is similar to the external one, and that there is nothing worthwhile behind either of them.

This is the reason why the inner community always lives hidden and in secret, in order to escape the many persecutions from the two other circles. You can cross paths with a member of our Brotherhood-Sisterhood every day without realizing it.

The Numerous Invisible Incarnations of Christ

There have been many incarnations of Christ, through a Master of the same stature as Jesus, in the school of St. John; and yet, the world never knew of this because those Masters did not create external churches. This is the case for Christian Rose+Cross. So the world has totally ignored their presence and their actions during the evolution of humanity.

Nobody has been able to find writings about the Cathars or

the Knights Templar; everything about them remains mysterious, yet no one can deny their existence, nor the formidable spiritual influence that they exercised, in many subtle ways, over humanity. At the basis of these currents, there were highly enlightened Teachers, who remain nameless. This is equally true of Freemasonry, which is the origin of democracy and has, therefore, had a tremendous influence on society.

This living current of Christ, which animated all of these groups, all of these authentic initiatic schools, is still present in humanity.

The schools have disappeared, and some people try to continue their teaching in an external way; but the school of Christ is living and shows itself in the present moment. It comes through the youngest and everyone can participate in it; you just have to understand the law of vibratory similitude. Turn your inner vibratory frequency towards Christ, towards the good and worthy man, towards the sun of the human soul, towards universal and selfless good; and you will meet us. If this book is in your hands, it is because a process has begun already. Many people reach the inner stream of the Rose+Cross without really realizing it; then they leave it, and thereby miss the chance that was offered to them.

The Necessity For a Universal Human Culture

Humanity is now living through a period of great change because all of the ancient systems of belief are crumbling and a global awareness is appearing. That is why the modern school of St. John tries to convey a truly universal teaching which can help all human beings—whatever their ethnic group, religion, etc. Behind this is a desire to plant the seeds of a future universal solar culture.

At the moment, the world does not have a universal culture; there are, instead, many cultures, linked to countries and peoples. However, the cosmic intelligence and the earthly intelligence are pushing humans towards the realization of a universal culture; and there could be many wars in the future if humans do not open themselves up to the solar teaching of the humanity of light.

Dear friend on the path of life, the words spoken here are esoteric, and, therefore, it is not easy to understand and assimilate them, because, in our contemporary world, we are not used to thinking in this way; for this reason, we must make an effort. These words show the presence in the world of initiatic teaching, which guides humanity in an invisible way. Everyone can better understand why the holy Brotherhood-Sisterhood of the Rose+Cross has remained inaccessible to the curious and the desecrators, but that it welcomes with open arms all of the well-intentioned, sincere and honest beings who call upon it with the aim of serving the will of the All-High for the good of all beings.

Do you hear the call?

All one has to do is open the door
to realize that, behind limited things,
there exists a world without limits.
You have this experience every day
when you walk out of your home.

The Inner Experiences of a Student of the Modern Rose+Cross

The Method of Infinity

If you wish to become a disciple of Christ, of the Johannite humanity—that is to say, if you wish to get closer to the enlightened man: the free, good, creative man; if you wish to develop all of the gifts hidden within you and walk on the path of enrichment, happiness, joy, true success and immortality; if you aspire to have the sacred and luminous knowledge of the Masters of the solar earth of Shamballa, of the celestial Jerusalem; and, above all, if you wish to make a complete success of your life on earth—then, starting now, listen to the universal wisdom of the worlds living within you, enter the secret chamber of your heart, and start your apprenticeship. Begin to study life!

Great is the school of life! It shines throughout all the universe. It can be found, in its complete form, in the whole of infinity, as well as in the different parts composing the universe.

When you think of life, think also of infinity, of the limitless and the formless. Consciously install this idea of infinity within your mind and allow it to carry you off into its realm; let it expand you and open you up, and then unite it with life.

The body cannot live without food, or without the process of breathing; likewise, the soul wastes away and becomes weak without this communion with the idea of infinity.

In this infinite space, think also of the unity of the cosmos: the cosmos is a whole. Feel this, and then imagine the sacred stream of life flowing from the love of the spirit and filling infinity.

A disciple turns towards the blue sky or the starlit sky, and, while thinking of infinite space, unites with universal life. Those who have never communed with the angel of infinity cannot understand the meaning of life, of the universe, of creation.

People can be taught in many different ways, including brainwashing; we, however, have chosen the method of infinity, which awakens and nourishes the soul and the mind, which moves in the direction of life.

Climb to the top of a mountain or a high building, or stand before the ocean, and consciously think about the idea of infinity; feel this idea within you and live this sensation fully. When you have had this experience and you know its vibration, you can call upon it and put yourself back into it whenever you want to. Infinity is limitless; it is permanently available to you.

Man will experience illness, stress, problems and negativity in his life on earth. This is because he has lost the key to the gate of infinity, of his soul, which is one with the cosmos and all the beings in it.

Man is not separate from the cosmos and the others—quite the opposite; man lives in the cosmos and the cosmos lives in him. Whether he is aware of it or not, man's place is not in the limited form of his physical body. He is much bigger, much vaster than that, and he suffocates in his body.

It is for this reason that, at night, he goes back towards his cosmic land, into space, and the infinite light.

The Angel of Infinity and the Force of Good

This kingdom of infinity is closed to the cruel and the selfish, because only the force of universal good is limitless. Evil carries within itself its own limitation.

You will recognize true good by the fact that it opens the gate of infinity within you.

Evil can only live in limited things. The vibration of infinity, when it is known and lived, confers the power to enlarge or to diminish things. So man learns to reduce the evil and increase the good in life. This is a very great science, even if it seems simplistic in its wording.

The angel of infinity is a great guide of light because it allows human beings to know the force of good.

If you put hate, death, fear or destruction in front of the notion of the limitless, of infinity, you immediately feel that this is not desirable and does not go in the direction of life, of a healthy and harmonious evolution.

If you put love, wisdom or goodness there, you have a strong feeling that this is right and true.

If you put creativity, liberty or inner enlightenment there, you feel that this also is right and true; but, at the same time, there appears the fundamental notion of responsibility.

Cosmic Responsibility

If, to the perception of infinity, you join the notion of responsibility, you have found the path of the school of divine life and you are walking towards us, towards the light which we serve;

and you benefit from all our encouragement and best wishes.

Faced with the infinite in everything, man must be responsible.

If the soul of man is as vast as the universe and if the cosmos lives in him, then man must be responsible for Everything.

If people do not cultivate this cosmic responsibility, they are abandoning, at the same time, the soul, their freedom, their creativity and their life; and they are losing the greatest source of help along the path.

Feeling responsible for the universe and for all beings—in one's thoughts, feelings, life and actions—is a wonderful and indescribable feeling, which carries man forward. This is the true meaning of Christ's words: *"I am in you and you are in me; and where I go, you go."*

One cannot understand mantric words like these if one is not part of the soul of the Johannite current, that is to say, if one has not experienced, in a fully living way, the vibration of the unity of the cosmos, of infinity and of responsibility.

The cosmos is one, and all of the conflicts that we may notice in it, and even in our lives, are not fundamental opposites, but more a quest for harmony, attempts at a universal harmonization of all beings. If you carry this vision within you, you will notice very quickly that forces are coming towards you from the infinite cosmos—that is, from all parts—to support you and help you in life.

It is man himself who, by his erroneous conceptions and habits in life, closes the doors to the celestial influences that wish to help and bless him.

People turn towards the divine only when they reach a dead end—or when they feel really lost, destroyed, at the end of their rope—because they know deep down that the infinite can do anything if one opens oneself up to it in the right way. But this is not the way that one attains mastery and initiation, because God is not the servant of man; it is man who must become the servant of good, of the sublime, of the Whole. If the relationships between things are correct, then everything is in order; but when the relationships are distorted, nothing works anymore.

Man, who is not even capable of putting his own life in order, would like to give orders to the cosmic intelligence. It is a good thing that this kind of rowdy character is limited; otherwise, what chaos, what disorder, there would be in the universe!

Man must turn towards the cosmic intelligence to become its disciple, its servant; and that is how he will manage to establish celestial order deep within himself and in his life.

Thus, the notion of responsibility awakens the concept of being a servant of life, of the celestial order.

The disciple does not want to damage the Whole and he

feels strongly within that he is still imperfect; so he starts to serve divine life and, through it, finds the path to perfection. It is by becoming this kind of servant that one finds the way to become a Master of love and wisdom, a free cosmic creator.

Others who believe that they are masters or kings, but who do not know infinity and who are irresponsible, are, in reality, slaves—servants of the personality, of anarchy, of the beast.

When man fulfills his personal responsibility in relation to his family, his word, his friends, that is already a very beautiful thing; but it is only the beginning of the awareness of the divine and saintly individuality of the worthy man. The disciple must open up to the vibration, the dimension, of cosmic responsibility.

The World Is the Way You Look At It

The perception of infinity is not something physical or material, but, rather, a spiritual experience which belongs to the domain of the soul. Every being of good will who so desires can feel infinity and, in this way, make an initial contact with their soul.

Man can study many things on earth; but, if he wants to approach what is essential in life, he must get to know the infinite, the supreme, the sublime. This is a process which must be conscious and voluntary. The person aspiring to the sublime must consciously form within this thought of infinity.

He consciously thinks:

Infinity—Infinity—Infinity

I think of you,

I feel you,

I live you.

That is when a transformation of his inner vibration will take place, because the psychic energy follows the thought. This is a law that everyone can and must freely experience: those who think about light draw it to them and create it around them. Those who think of darkness do the same, and help to spread throughout the world the heavy clouds of discontentment, doubt and fear which slow down the evolution of beings. Why take on the useless burden of dark thoughts and feelings?

Man wants to suffer because, in his ignorance, he has tied himself to dark energies, and now he clings to them out of habit. This attitude slows down the evolution of human life.

Life is perpetually moving; it goes forward, it rises up towards the spiritual summits.

If man refuses the transformation required by life, as is often the case, if he clings to his prejudices and established ideas, he then, in an unconscious way, introduces illnesses into the soul of humanity.

This is why it is said that "life smiles upon the audacious." It is the audacious, the innovators, who have brought the blessings of heaven to humanity.

Life does not like immobility; this is the energy of death, which wants to stop everything. In his thought, in his inner life, in his consciousness, man can progress, can rise all the way up to infinity.

Those who refuse this are clinging to the power of death, which they help to spread on earth. But it is clear that, the more life and consciousness grow, the more man shines and understands the mysteries of creation.

Today people are educated in such a way that they only believe in the world of visible shapes; so, for them, everything is limited, everything has an end. And, therefore, death is the logical conclusion. This kind of conception or vision of life can only destroy or deform humanity. Humans are good at putting up boundaries, cages, inside which they lock themselves. In reality, even if boundaries are useful on earth, there is nothing to stop us from crossing them, from time to time, and expanding our horizon—like the astronaut who, looking down on earth from space, marveled at the sight and said that, from his point of view, he did not see any boundaries between countries.

So everything is a question of conception. From our point

of view, the evolution of consciousness and of life is limitless. Thus, everything becomes joyful; we enter into the vibration of Everything possible, everything good. Carrying around this kind of belief, one notices that the cosmos responds to it and opens up a new horizon, a new path, for man. So the world is the way you look at it. If your eyes are fixed only on the visible, on forms, you think that everything is limited, and you see in space only emptiness, nothingness.

If your eyes are fixed on life in movement, you understand that there is no empty space, and you grasp the meaning of eternity and perfectibility.

The Perception of Universal Life

The power of life is unlimited, and it resides in every being. If you use this power to affirm that you are nothing, to limit yourself, then it will do so; but, if you use it to affirm yourself, in the sacred stream of life, as an evolving being, then you will become aware of that fact.

All beings carry this power of life within them; and one of the spiritual exercises of the disciple is to become aware of, to practice, seeing life in its essence. We will have the occasion to come back to this subject; but, for the moment, we have to say that he must succeed in perceiving life as present in its totality—in the limitless Whole, as well as in the different parts. This is an inner vision, which must be developed while meditating. In this way, every thing and every being becomes a carrier of life, and not only of its own life; it contains the potential for Everything possible, the absolute, the infinite. This is how the disciple can be led to suddenly realize that a simple, little speck of dust flying through the air is related to the totality of the cosmos, which surrounds, and carries within it, the absolute, the sublime, the infinite. Then he understands Christ's words: *"Are not two sparrows sold for an ace? Yet not one of them will fall to the ground without our Father knowing it! And what of you, then? Even every hair on your head is counted!"*

After learning to concentrate on infinity in the Whole and infinity in the parts, the disciple starts to perceive life, the links which unite the parts to each other, and the parts of the Whole; he has entered the school of divine life. Through this training, the disciple sees developing within him the sense of respect for life in general, and for the life of all beings in particular.

Because life is one at its source and remains one in spite of all of its apparent divisions, the disciple also acquires the sense of the universal Brotherhood-Sisterhood.

These are very important acquisitions and stages in the life and evolution of the soul.

The disciple realizes, moreover, that the source of the one

life is the love of God, and that, because of the life within him, he is never separated from God and his limitless love. But man must not move towards the love of God in a passive way; he must actively do something beautiful and divine with his life, and thus become a worthy creator of this divine life within him.

A Rose+Cross Exercise: God, the Great All

Find a place out in nature, or at home, where you feel good and calm.

Get into a comfortable position, making sure that the spine remains straight.

Allow your breathing to become deep, regular and calm.

Be completely calm, peaceful, relaxed.

Consciously place the weight of your body on the ground and let yourself be carried by the earth.

Next, place all of the weight of your interior and exterior life on the ground, and get a momentary taste of rest and tranquillity.

When you have reached this state of rest, awaken your consciousness in the silence, the sensitivity, the delicacy and the subtlety which live in and around you.

Now, concentrate on this thought:

The totality around me,
The totality within me,
God, the great All.

Concentrating on the thought means that you consciously think the mantric words "The totality around me", and, at the same time, you try to awaken your consciousness in the perception of this reality.

You try to perceive, to experience, to verify, with every fiber of your being, the reality of these words.

It is necessary to concentrate on them mentally; through thought, you must find the totality around you. When this thought has been obtained in a concrete way, you must try to feel it with your heart. Of course, this is absolutely not easy and can require a lot of practice; but, if you succeed at it, you will be transformed.

The same holds true for the mantric words "The totality within me". If you succeed in feeling them and living them as a spiritual experience, you will be transformed; you will discover inside yourself a space as vast as the universe—that is, limitless, infinite. Moreover, you will be able to discover that this spiritual space is not empty, but that it is inhabited by beings, and that it potentially contains all beings. These experiences are very difficult to describe, and one must live them oneself to progress on the path.

The Mysteries of the Great Universe, the Small Universe, and the Divine

When the disciple concentrates on the totality around him, then within him, he perceives that this is an extraordinary reality, but that there is still a duality in it.

When he concentrates on the words "God, the great All", he rises up into unity, into a higher, unique, synthetic, reality. This reality unites the other two and contains them in itself alone.

Through the first mantric words, the disciple can experience macrocosmic consciousness.

With the second, it is microcosmic consciousness; and, finally, through the last words, he can experience divine consciousness, the supreme, unity.

In this simple exercise of the current of the Rose+Cross of St. John and of the circle of light of the Masters of the Cosmic Tradition, there is limitless knowledge.

Indeed, man was created to elevate himself to the knowledge of the mysteries of the great universe, the small universe, and the divine. All of the experiences of his daily life lead him to, and prepare him for, this knowledge. It was to point out this great goal that the Greek hierophants said to the neophytes: *"Man, know yourself"* (microscomic consciousness), *"and you will know the universe"* (macrocosmic consciousness), *"and God"* (divine consciousness).

During the day, man experiences himself as a microcosmos; and it is at night, in his sleep, that he ventures out and expands into the cosmos. Likewise, he incarnates on the earth to have the living experience of the personality, and passes through the gate of death to return to the cosmos. This whole process goes round and round in an endless circle, until man awakens to the reality of the exercise which we have just given.

In this circle of days and nights, man is always a divided being; on one side, he has the self-awareness of the body but he does not have the cosmic awareness of his spirit, and, on the other side, this is reversed.

It is this situation which creates all unhappiness and problems, because it is said that a divided kingdom is destined to suffer.

Without macrocosmic consciousness, man cannot understand the meaning of life; and, without divine consciousness, he does not have the means to accomplish the task of his physical embodiment. This is why initiation is the primordial act for life on earth. Without it, man is not aware of the importance of this life in a physical body, and is content just to live passively and to let himself go.

Man, Be What You Are!

For example, man can express himself very well, have opinions about spirituality, or even on humanitarian subjects. But, basically, all of that remains external and does not really interest him; because, in his actions, he thinks only of himself, of his own person, or else he acts like a materialist.

So man is divided even in his personality, which is a reflection of the great division between cosmic consciousness and earthly consciousness.

Likewise, a man can speak very convincingly about the beauty of platonic love and, in his private life, jump on every woman who comes near him, with other ideas in his head or somewhere else. On the other hand, a man can remain silent about humanitarian actions or platonic love, but practice it naturally in his life because that is what he is.

We often want things that we think we do not have, and, thus, we neglect the hidden gifts which are within us. Man is much richer than he believes himself to be; and, to discover this, he must not try to be what he is not, but, rather, what he is.

There are, within us, sublime angelic forces which desire to burst out, to express themselves and to surprise us. So let's allow ourselves to be surprised by the beauty of the Holy Spirit, who lives within us, and let's give him the freedom to express himself.

Man does not need to make an effort to be what he is; he simply is it, and, therefore, does not think about it or pay attention to it.

But what really interests the Masters of the school of St. John, and of initiatic Christianity, is, precisely, what one is; and they direct the attention of their students towards this state of being. The student must first look at himself, as he is in his personality, and accept himself totally, with his faults as well as his qualities. Having faults is not serious; it is simply necessary to recognize them and accept them, and to start walking on the path. After a while, the student starts to perceive, behind his personality, the gleamings of the superior self, of God, the great All; and then, discovering his true nature, all he has to do is master his earthly personality so that it manifests only the impulses of his true, divine, nature. He has to think like God Himself, feel like Him, and, finally, act in total cosmic harmony with his true nature of man of light, of son-daughter of God.

This is the initiation which the School of Life and Spirit and the current of St. John tries to develop in its students.

TO BE ONE'S TRUE NATURE, TO CONSCIOUSLY FEEL DIVINE UNITY AND TO INCARNATE IT THROUGH THE PERSONALITY, THAT IS THE HIGHEST INITIATION.

But humans, in order to become conscious in the physical body, only think and feel their personalities; they do not incarnate them. They live their lives without knowing who they really are.

The Light of the True Man

The mantric formula: "The totality around me; the totality within me; God, the Great All" must make the student become aware that he is a living, independent and free being who carries within him all of the infinite possibilities of life, and, therefore, that his future in his hands; also, that he carries within him all of the beings of the cosmos, and that he, therefore, has an influence on them; then, finally, that he carries within him the divine, and that he has an influence on its harmonious manifestation on earth.

If man neglects this divine aspect, then, at the same time, he is condemning the man within himself and, consequently, the man in all men, because man cannot be without the divine, without spirituality.

It is only in and through spirituality that man takes on his whole dimension, his entire value, and that he can succeed in mastering matter; otherwise, it is matter that masters and destroys him.

Through this work, we are going to try to go deeper into this question of the essential being of man, and to give concrete and practical exercises for initiatic apprenticeship, so that man may seize the sacred stream of life and become the creator of his divine future.

The aspiration of the disciple must be to find the path of the man of light, of his true being. This man of light realized by Christ is the gate to the kingdom of unity, of the great Whole. Man is no longer divided and separated; he is one with the Whole in his consciousness and his life. Christ, the spirit of the sun, came to bring to humans this state of being of man, and it is the task of the school of St. John to realize it. It is not enough just to think of this state, nor even to feel it; you must be it, incarnate it in the reality of the earth and of the physical body. To help with this, we have, through the workshops of the School of Life and Spirit, given a dance of the Cosmic Tradition which permits the incarnation of Christ on earth and in humanity. (1)

---

(1) We must point out that this chapter and the following one are very closely tied to this sacred dance taught by Christ on Mount Tabor, in the bosom of his internal School, and revived by Olivier Manitara in the current of St. John.

Many explanations given throughout this chapter find their ending and their practical realization in the dance of the man of light. Please consult the teachings of the School of Life and Spirit founded by Olivier Manitara. (Editor's Note).

This involves a great and sacred science which belongs to those whose consciousness is awakened and who aspire to work for infinite Good, for the Whole.

Going Deeper Into the Exercise

While you are thinking "The totality around me", you can become aware that you are tying yourself to the macrocosmos. You can then concentrate on the four elements, the minerals, the vegetation, the animals, the humans, the planets and the stars that are bathing in the infinite space carried by life.

While you are thinking "The totality within me", you can try to find within yourself everything that exists in the universe.

For example, the physical body for minerals, the body of life and of reproduction for vegetables, the body of warmth and of feelings for animals, the body of thoughts for humans, etc. It is through this type of exercise that we can approach the knowledge of the global man as taught by the school of St. John and the light of the Cosmic Tradition.

Now, you can advance more in your meditation; when you concentrate on "the totality around you" and you look at a human being, fix yourself on him, on his physical form. You can see that form, just as you can look at the form of an animal or an object. But if you try to look at what is behind it, you can discover the personality, composed of the affinities and the karma of the being. Looking further, you can contemplate the immortal soul and, finally, the divine creative spirit. You can have this experience with an animal, a tree or a stone, and the result will be basically the same, but full of valuable lessons.

If you really want to progress in your study of the teaching of the initiates, it is not enough just for you to know that this exercise exists; you must perform it, to be able to extract its quintessence.

The task of the School of Life and Spirit, with its initiatic workshops, is to prepare beings, in liberty, to live exercises like these on their own. This is a help on the path to a healthy and serene life.

The Action of the Cosmos on Man and Self-Awareness

You can perceive, through this experience, that the physical body is elaborate, built according to the model of the etheric body. This etheric body is subject to the influence of the whole cosmos, which is engraved on it. So you can see that the whole cosmos has an effect on the body of man. In addition, you can discern the astral soul, which also acts on the etheric body or soul. This astral soul is spread throughout all the planets; it carries the karma of the being, and thus imprints a direction on the etheric body, which influences the destiny of man incarnated on earth. This influence can slow down or increase the action of the cosmos, which affects the physical body.

Behind the astral soul, you can discover the image of the true man, which lives in the sun.

This image, by reflecting itself in the etheric and physical body of man, gives him self-awareness, the awareness of being an "I".

However, when one is awake, self-awareness is only a deformed reflection, like a film projected onto a screen through a cloud of smoke. What deforms the awareness of the pure self manifested by this spiritual sun is the astral-mental soul situated between it and the etheric-physical.

If you look more closely at this spiritual sun of the "I-Am", you will discover that it is one with the cosmos, that it is the spiritual self of the cosmos, and that it is what gives man his own self-awareness.

At night, man leaves his etheric-physical shell and expands out into the kingdom of the stars, according to karmic affinities.

The disciples, through the practice of certain exercises, try to rise towards the "I-Am" sun, to receive impulses from it, and to then transmit them to the daytime consciousness. The whole task of a disciple is to know this divine self, in order to act under its influence, through his mental-astral soul, in order to make an imprint on his etheric-physical body. In this way, he can take part in the direction of his destiny and become a free creator within the will of the One-All.

The Initiatic Experience of the Tree

If you now concentrate, in the same way, on an animal, a tree or a stone, you will make other discoveries. In the initiatic process, this experience of spiritual vision is often realized with a tree.

Some beings who did not know about the solar teaching of the Cosmic Tradition, but who prayed to God fervently every day to become better, have lived this experience of going out of themselves while in prayer, to go and fuse with a tree in the area. There they discovered marvelous secrets, secrets of the soul, and links which unite beings and things.

This is why one finds the tree mentioned in the traditions of all peoples.

The mysteries that we are talking about here are very difficult to explain, because there are no words to articulate the spiritual and all of the consequences of initiatic experiences on the life of man. That is why we ask you to give us all of your attention, and to have a very warm and understanding heart.

The Encounter Between Nathanael and Christ

In St. John's gospel, there is an allusion to this initiatic experience of the tree when the Master Jesus goes to find his first disciples. Jesus sees Nathanael coming towards him, and says about him: *"Here, truly, is a straightforward Israelite."* Nathanael asked: *"Where did you get to know me?"* Jesus answered him: *"Before Philip called you, when you were under the fig tree, I saw you."* Nathanael replied: *"Master, you are the son of God, you are the king of Israel."* Jesus answered him: *"Because I told you I saw you under the fig tree, you believe! You will see better yet."* And he said again: *"In truth, in truth, I tell you, you will see the sky open and the angels of God rise and descend above the son of man."*

Five minutes earlier, Nathanael had been criticizing the Master Jesus, saying: *"Can anything good come out of Nazareth?"*—that is, out of the Essene community and teaching. Everyone, at that time, knew that Jesus was an Essene teacher.

The Master simply tells him that he saw him under the fig tree; and he is immediately converted and proclaims that Jesus is the son of God—that is, that in him lives the spiritual sun, the cosmic "I-Am", which the initiates could only contemplate at night in a consciousness of awakened dreams.

In reality, Nathanael is an initiate, and the experience of the fig tree is an initiatic stage in the secret teaching of the Israelite tradition.

Through this initiation, the disciple was able to enlarge his life-consciousness to the point of fusing with the spiritual life of a tree, and then with that of an entire people. It is for this reason that the Master says of him: *"Here is a true Israelite"*, and that he links this fact to the fig tree. Through this initiation, the disciple was able, not only to commune with the soul of the people, the angels and the archangels who direct it, but in addition, the life of all the ancestors of this people—all the way back to Abraham, back to Adam and Eve—was also revealed to him.

All of these beings were living as a memory in the astral-mental soul of the people. Reaching back to Adam and Eve, the first couple of the people of Israel, the disciple could contemplate the spiritual sun behind them, the being who had said to Moses on Mount Sinai: *"I am the I-Am."*

After living this initiation, Nathanael found himself facing the Master Jesus, the Nazarene, and recognized in him the solar being of his initiation, the being who lived before Adam, the cosmic Self of the universe—and that being living in a conscious, awakened man who could speak to him, saying: *"In truth, I say to you..."*

Because of his initiation, Nathanael was able to understand that this "I" was not the "I" of the mortal person of the man, but that this person had given up its place to the cosmic "I", who is the king of Israel, the king of all beings, the king of the universe.

Thus, in this being—Jesus—the celestial order was reestablished; the kingdom of God, the Solar Culture, the Trinosophy-Synarchy of the Rose+Cross triumphed and opened up a new path for man.

Because, even if the initiates, like Nathanael, were able to have a spiritual vision of the divine sun and to live in the soul of their people, they were not consciously participating in all of these mysteries. Then, suddenly, the Master brings a new and deeply moving spiritual impulse that allows man to consciously participate in the mystery of divinity and in the evolution of the cosmos.

Man Carries Within Him the Future of the Cosmos

It is remarkable to realize that the first people to understand Christ, the enlightened man, were the initiates, those who had been preparing themselves for centuries by following the teaching of the holy divine mysteries.

Humans, in their pride and their vanity, think that, if Christ stood in front of them, they would recognize him at first glance and would understand him as soon as he started to speak, without needing to prepare themselves, to make an effort; but the mysteries of life show us that this is not true.

The Master describes to Nathanael an initiation that is even greater and more vast than his: the individual man, through his personality, becomes the carrier of all beings, of the whole cosmos, and of the divine.

The open sky tells us about the mysteries of the evolution of the cosmos which are linked to the etheric-physical body of man.

Man carries within his etheric-physical body the future of the cosmos. That is why the angels of God—that is, the intelligent life at work in nature—work on the son of man.

The son of man symbolizes the man-personality which is made in the image of the cosmos and of the divine; and this is linked to the mystery of the astral-mental body and of the "I-Am" sun, which we have already talked about.

Exercise Based on the Words of Christ to Nathanael

Prepare yourself for meditation, for your spiritual work, by following the indications given in the book *The Secret Teaching on Breathing in the School of St. John*, or the instructions given in the teachings-by-correspondence for the preparation of initiation.

Everything inside you is calm, pure and clear.

Concentrate on the words of Christ: *"You will see the sky open and the angels of God rise and descend above the son of man."*

Think these words very deeply; bring them to life within you. The open sky means that it has become, in a way, transparent, and that, through it, you can see life in movement. This life in movement is the angels.

You can see them through the air, the earth, water, fire, flowers, etc.

The son of man is you; and all the angels can come into contact with you, work with you to guide you in the harmonious direction of evolution. You, too, as the son of man, carrier of the consciousness and the life of the "I-Am", can consciously take part in this great angelic work.

Try to feel all of this in your meditation, and to end your work by sending good thoughts, good feelings and good wishes to all the beings who, like you, are working for the light, and the healthy and serene evolution of every being.

Knowledge of the Macrocosmos: I Am One With the Tree

Thinking again about this experience of the tree of life, we realize that we can find it in the secret teachings of the Druids, of Judaism, of the Egyptian priests, of Buddhism, of Islam, of

Mazdeism, of Taoism, etc. It is a universal symbol, which, therefore, comes from the Cosmic Tradition.

The disciple was to meditate under a tree and concentrate his thoughts only on it. All of the thoughts and imaginings not related to the tree were to be, progressively, eliminated. This could take weeks, even months, of training and perseverance—until the day when the disciple felt the particular sensation of no longer seeing the tree from the outside, but from the inside. He had the impression of living in the soul of the tree, of knowing it in its intimate life; he felt, more and more, in a state of unity with the essence of the tree, and discovered, to his great surprise, that he was the tree, and that the tree was him, inside his soul. He had not become the tree through his long and profound meditation; no, it had always been this way, only he did not know it, or, rather, he had forgotten about it, he was no longer aware of it.

So, what lives outside of man, in its form, also lives inside the soul of man, in a subtle and spiritual way.

What the disciple of the ancient mysteries could acquire through such experiences can be summarized in the knowledge of the microcosmos. But now Christ says that the sky is going to open up and that the contemplation of the angels of God, and of their rapport with men, is going to be known; this involves a knowledge of the macrocosmos, and of its relationships to man on earth. In this way, Christ teaches that man on earth must learn to live in cosmic harmony and unison, and not just for himself, with a selfish goal, nor even for a particular people, but for the Whole; because that is the meaning and the will of the one-life.

The Law of Love and the Circle of Light of the Cosmic Tradition

If man does not understand and does not go in the direction of life, he will experience suffering, pain and death, because that is the law. There is only one law in the cosmos which is valid for every being, and that is the law of life, which is one with love.

Man on earth can live in harmony with this law, and, in that case, he enters the circle of magnetic light of the Cosmic Tradition; or else in disharmony with it, and then he constructs his own unhappiness with every unjust thought and action.

As a living being, man is a creator, through his thoughts, feelings and will. If his creations are in disharmony with love, he builds around himself a prison, which will progressively cut him off from the celestial streams and destroy him.

The School of Life and Spirit wants man to learn to live on earth with a perfect understanding of the customs of the Cosmic Tradition.

The Technique of the Open Sky and the Great Meditation of the Self

When Christ speaks of the "open sky", it means that the disciple must not be content with superficial knowledge, which allows him to perceive only the surface of things; he must develop the penetrating vision of the eagle, which knows how to look at what is behind the forms.

In this way, the disciple always sees the tree on which he is concentrating; but one can say that, at the same time, the tree has opened up to allow a spiritual reality to appear. What he has learned from the tree, he can now experience, in the same way, with the sky, with other people, and with everything that surrounds him.

He can also do the same with everything that lives within him—his thoughts, feelings, habits, etc.

This is the golden key of knowledge: the direct perception of the spiritual side of beings and things. It is man himself who serves as an instrument for this knowledge.

When man has the experience of seeing the one-life behind things, his thoughts, feelings, desires, and everything that makes up his personality on earth, will become for him not a goal (having a personality) but a way to show beauty, truth and nobility on earth. What ordinary humans call their "self" becomes for him an instrument, like the brush that the painter uses to spread the colors. For the disciple the colors are the thoughts, feelings and aspirations circulating around the self.

If, instead of taking the tree as a point of concentration, the disciple meditates on his own self in such a way that it becomes "transparent", opening up to reveal what lives behind it, he will make some interesting discoveries; and he will be transformed.

Of course, to practice such meditations, you must have a lot of perseverance; and it is especially preferable to be guided and supported.

This has always been the mission of the guides and instructors in the light.

The Path of True Happiness

The first discovery that man can make is that he does not know himself. He knows his self only in relation to something exterior, but he has not found the self in its spiritual essence.

If the disciple pursues his investigation, he will be led to live the experience of St. John the Baptist: *"He who comes after me will rank ahead of me because, before me, he was."*

These extraordinary words are spoken by he who has understood that the real nature of the human self lies beyond the physical body, and even beyond the mortal personality. At this level, if the disciple has not yet succeeded in fusing with the superior self, which is God Himself, he has at least seen it and understood that, by walking towards this vision, he will obtain amazing and sublime results.

Behind the personality that carries the small self, there is the great All, the divine, the I-Am.

Man can think this, even feel it, and still remain outside of this holy temple, which is the unique reality, the unique truth which breathes life into everything.

An authentic initiatic School wants only one thing for its students—to have them attain the sublime light.

When he is born on earth, man and the cosmos build a personality which carries a self, and the man who identifies with it is no longer himself; he is only the shadow of his own reality. A disciple recognizes this whole process, and sees how this fake personality was created; he learns to identify with the true eternal self, and strives to control the forces of his personality, so that they will serve his true self. Only man himself can accomplish this work, and re-establish celestial order within himself.

The cosmic intelligence has placed inside of man, and around him, all of the right conditions to enable him to reach his goal—harmony between his two natures, between the sky and the earth, between his internal sky and earth. When he succeeds at this, he will know true happiness and fulfillment.

Ignorant people can pray for hours for an end to war in the world, while finding it normal to remain at war within themselves.

The cosmic intelligence will not listen to such prayers because what it wants is to have man draw conclusions from the trials and the joys that he is called to live through. For the cosmic intelligence, trials are not negative; they are materials, an energy that man must know how to use. If he does not know how to use this energy, then he will suffer; and it is through this suffering that he will learn progressively. By directly adopting the knowledge of the initiates, one avoids a lot of unnecessary worries.

The Disciple Must Want to Live the Experience of the Inner Light

If one looks at these mysteries objectively, one arrives at the conclusion that man cannot know his true being in the physical plane, because this plane is directly dependent on the forces that rule the personality.

The physical sphere is a means, a support which allows us to rise up towards the superior. It is because they are ignorant of this fact that most humans live on earth without ever having the experience of the inner light, of the spiritual sun of the soul.

The Rosicrucian Students' Secret Exercises

In the stream of the Rose+Cross—that is, in the pure and holy teaching of Johannite Christianity—the student is led to do this exercise of contemplating the plant world. He is asked to observe a dead tree; then a tree in winter; next, a budding tree; and, finally, a tree covered with leaves, flowers and fruit.

Of course, he must not be satisfied to look only with his eyes, but also with the force of perception of the heart and of life. He is asked to look at life—to feel the invisible, the intangible.

After this, he must meditate, in the same way, on a dead man, a sleeping man, and a man who is awakened in the physical sphere.

He can also take the example of a pebble, a grain of wheat and a stalk of wheat.

It is important that the disciple have these experiences himself; however, we can say a few words on this subject, in order to progress further in the spiritual practice that we wish to provide as a help along the way.

The first realization that he can come to is that, from the physical point of view, the man, or the tree—whether dead, sleeping or alive—remains the same; what changes between these different states of being resides essentially in the spiritual manifestation.

We must immediately state here that what may seem simple and obvious to us takes on another dimension entirely when the disciple makes this realization in his meditation.

If we are talking about these exercises, which have remained secret for centuries, it is precisely because the simple thoughts which flow from them possess the power, if they are received in the right way, to develop in man organs which allow him to have access to the spiritual world and to initiatic knowledge.

The Mystery of the Grain of Wheat

Our Rose+Cross student can also discover that the dead tree has become like a mineral; its plant life has left it. It is this plant life that makes the difference between a grain of wheat and a pebble.

Like the pebble, the grain of wheat can stay at rest for centuries; but as soon as it is planted in the earth, and nurtured by the sun and water, it sprouts, and the power of life unfolds.

Keeping these thoughts in mind, our student starts to see the life in the pebble as an enveloping energy, and the life in the grain of wheat as containing the form of the future stalk.

If he looks, in this way, at a grain planted in the earth, he grasps what Christ, through the Master Jesus, was saying: *"The angels of God were rising and descending above him."*

Looking at a man in the same way, he sees in his heart this same grain of wheat containing the etheric image of the solar man, the future man.

He understands that, if man discovers how to plant this grain, it will develop by itself.

We have already spoken a lot about theses mysteries in saying that a living community of free individualities, united in love and in the field of life of a true initiatic school, represents the good earth and the right conditions to awaken divine life in man.

Now, if the Holy Spirit will help us, we are going to give some movements of the Cosmic Tradition which permit the awakening in man of this grain of the man of light.

Let us now continue what we have started.

Life Is Hanging by a Thread

When our student of the holy, and forever pure and luminous, Order of the Rose+Cross looks at the dead tree, he sees that the tie to life is broken. Similarly, for a man, the tie uniting the living soul, the etheric body, to the physical body is cut. It is to point this out that popular clairvoyant wisdom says that *"life is hanging by a thread."*

What remains in the body is the cellular life, which starts to disintegrate; and then natural forces of decomposition appear.

The etheric body leaves; but, for the moment, we do not wish to go into that question. On the other hand, what our student learns, in a living way, is that life is, indeed, hanging by a thread, by a living link; and that, he can see.

If the tie is cut, the forces of decomposition appear; and the same is true for divine life. If man is not tied in a living way to the divine spirit within him, he looks alive to the world but, in reality, he is already being surrounded and penetrated by the forces of decomposition. It is not enough just to be alive in the physical body, in a biological way; we must also be alive in the spirit, and the divine source must flow within us. I have chosen the image of flowing water because it is precisely the one that our student can contemplate when he looks at a man in whom the Holy Spirit lives and shows itself.

For others, it is more a question of stagnant water. Man's water stagnates because he is too egoistical, too locked-up inside himself because he is afraid of everything, and full of distrust. By this attitude, he prevents inspiration, and the impulses of love, and renewal from penetrating inside him, so it is the putrid gases and the mosquitoes that move in; and, satisfied, he thinks: "At least things cannot get any worse."

The living link with the spirit, with the hierarchy of Christ, with Shamballa, and with the divine school, is a great reality which must not be underestimated.

When, on certain days, you feel an impulse of life, joy, love, clarity, and inspiration, it is because this link is radiating light. On the other hand, when you feel sad, in a bad mood, hopeless, irritable, and unhappy with yourself, it is because this link is thin and weak.

Try, then, to imagine it as a string of liquid silver, made of moving energy. It starts at the top of your head and goes all the way up to the sun. When it gets to the sun, it is filled with pure, divine energies, which it pours down onto you. Imagine the silver string getting wider and carrying a living, golden water which surrounds you and fills the center of the head, the heart, the stomach, and then the whole body.

This exercise allows one to practice the art of intensifying life. The one who knows how to intensify life knows the secret for enlarging the consciousness.

When the grain of wheat starts to sprout, it is because life is intensifying within it. Its body becomes too small to hold it, so new organs develop. This law also works for man; if he intensifies the pure, celestial, divine life within him, other organs will develop in him and he will be able to taste new perceptions, and to discover around him a new world and new possibilities which, up to then, had been totally invisible.

The Awakening of the Fire Snake of the Kundalini

When our student in the field of life of the Rose+Cross looks at a tree in winter, he finds that there is an analogy between it and the grain of wheat, or even a sleeping man. The sun and the cosmic forces have withdrawn, and it falls asleep.

Looking at a leafless tree in winter, we might think that it is dead; but, in reality, life is still working inside of it, in a kind of slow motion.

What makes the tree blossom in the spring is the renewed action of the sun and the atmosphere upon it.

The sun awakens the life, the etheric part, of the sleeping tree, animating it; and this revival of the tree's etheric body produces leaves, flowers and fruit on the physical tree.

This same phenomenon was observed in man, with great interest, by the initiates, and was described as the awakening of the wheels, the chakras, the lotus flowers, or the roses of light, in the etheric body. Or else, as the process of the rising of sap in the plant, like the rising of the power of the life hidden in the form, the power of the snake: the kundalini.

In the teaching of our oriental Brothers and Sisters, the kundalini is what we call the Telesma force, the strong force of all forces, the very power of the life which is asleep at the base of the spine and which begins its awakening in the heart, as we have indicated above.

Once this force has been awakened, it can move either upwards, and the disciple can attain the greatest spiritual development, or downwards, and this triggers the beginning of degeneration, because all of the lowest passions and vices are activated and multiplied. The powers of death and decomposition are thus intensified.

Therefore, you must take a lot of precautions if you wish to work with these divine energies; and, most importantly, you must really know what you are doing.

The exercises and methods of the School of Life and Spirit, of the Christian and Johannite mysteries of the Rose+Cross, are healthy and lead to a harmonious development.

It is futile to work on the awakening of these energies if you have not first lived the initiatic experiences with the plant world described here.

In a way, it is the intelligence of the plant world which must instruct the neophyte in these cosmic mysteries.

The one who feels within the force of the aspiration to the superior life, to the divine consciousness, to the absolute consciousness, must be careful and intelligent, and must always remember that preparation is the most important stage of initiation. When this preparation has reached the level of successfully controlling the thoughts, the heart, and the life, then everything happens naturally and harmoniously.

The Analogy Between the Sleeping Man and the Plant World

It is something extraordinary, for our student, to contemplate the dormant etheric life of a tree that awakens and comes to life under the spiritual action of the sun. There is an energy there, which starts to dance, to whirl around and to intersect, in order to give birth to the leaves.

So the student is led to have this thought: "The whole cosmos is working on this tree."

Looking at a sleeping man in the same way, he first sees a physical body lying on a bed—then, because of his training, the etheric body which gives it life. He then realizes that there is a real analogy between this man and a plant; the etheric body of the man is similar to plant life, and the same processes can take place in him. This is a great inner revelation for the student.

Of course, man's etheric life does not undergo the same cycle as that of plants, because what the sun does for the tree, the spirit of the sun does for man. The influence of the spirit of the sun on the etheric man gives birth to self-awareness inside him. In the morning, when he wakes up, his self animates the etheric-physical body once again. The disciple becomes aware that he can say "I am myself" and feel it because the spirit of the sun is imprinted on his etheric body.

This spirit does not live in the plant; and, for this reason, the plant does not have a personal self, but more a collective self: the physical sun. That is why plants grow, sleep and wake up all together, whereas man can sleep at any hour of the day.

We could discover other profound mysteries if we looked at procreation in plants, animals and humans.

Contemplating the Astral Soul

Between the etheric self and soul of man, the Rose+Cross student can contemplate the astral soul, which he finds between the plant and man in the animal, or between the plant and the sun in the atmosphere of the moon. This astral soul allows man to have feelings, likes and dislikes; and, at night, it propels him into the world of dreams, through which he can fuse with, and expand inside of, things and beings, to taste the inner life of the cosmos and of living nature. Of course, most humans are not aware of all of these processes because they have not developed the organs of perception which could reveal them to them. They are like trees in winter.

The Universe Is Alive, Just As I Am Alive

When the student performs these spiritual exercises of contemplation correctly, he perceives that, more and more, he is acquiring the ability to observe himself sleeping; and he is progressively led to live this experience, so difficult to express in words, that the universe is alive, just as the human being is alive. He has a living understanding of the great reality that everything is alive and gifted with intelligence, soul and spirit. And more than that, he experiences the knowledge that there is a close link between everything that exists and the cosmos, the great harmonious Whole.

For example, minerals are linked to the body of the cosmos, and plants to its living soul. They have their independent life, which is fixed around a center of manifestation; but on the other hand, it is the etheric soul of the cosmos, the great Whole, that lives within them, and through them. It is the same for animals, who are united to the cosmos' soul of desire and feeling, and for humans, who receive the intelligence, the solar self, of the cosmos. Above man, the angels carry the notion and the force of purity, transparency and service. The archangels are in communion with the intelligence and the action of the collective, fraternal, and communal forces.

Exercise for the Disciples of the Johannite Humanity: the Path to the Terra-Lucida, Shamballa

Imagine yourself in luminous white clothes; and make everything around you pure, harmonious, and clear.

First feel that your body is one with the body of the earth. Feel the earth as the body of the cosmos and your body as one with the earth.

Think, feel, live: "My body comes from the earth, it is she who formed it, it is she who carries it like a gentle, loving mother; and it is to her that it will return."

Through the air that you breathe, feel the breath of the earth, and, through her, that of the cosmos.

Through the blood which flows through your veins, nourishing your body, feel the blood of the earth: the streams, the rivers, the seas, which irrigate and fertilize the ground.

Through your bones and your skeleton, think and feel the rocks and stones of the mountains and the plains.

Through your nerves, feel the metallic veins of the earth and the currents of energy that are circulating.

Through all of your senses, feel how the earth awakens you to life.

Once you have really taken the time to feel this, concentrate on the life that circulates through, and animates, your whole body, the whole earth, all of space, the whole cosmos.

Bring to life, inside of you, this vision, this imagining of infinite life filling up space. The earth is suspended in this space, like other celestial bodies. Have a clear vision within you of the living earth floating in infinite space.

Now try to feel how the earth was created out of the substance of this infinite space, this cosmic ocean of life.

Think: "The creation of the world came from space; but the world could be destroyed, and space, and the place in which it resides, still would not disappear."

If the world was destroyed, if it returned to space, the place it had occupied would not be empty, because there is no emptiness; everything is filled with space, which is, itself, bathed in infinite life.

If you perform this exercise correctly, you will be able to live this experience of seeing the earth become transparent and of discovering, through it, the mysterious school of Agartha, then of Shamballa, and, also, the hierarchy of the Elohims, who created the earth and take care of it.

This is a powerful meditation for finding the path to St. John's kingdom: Shamballa, the land of the living.

You will also be able to see your body become transparent and the etheric soul, with these cosmic mysteries, appear behind it.

The one who reaches the etheric body can understand that

life is the most important thing because "it is life that gives life and words have nothing to do with it"; words are only the tools of life, which carries the spirit within it.

The etheric body contains the greatest mysteries of the cosmos because, without life, nothing is. Life is the highest divine manifestation and, with it, we can obtain everything, because life contains Everything possible. The one who knows how to work with life is on the path of light.

The Astral Soul Carries All Visible and Invisible Animals

Once you have really taken the time to feel all of this, concentrate your thoughts on the personality inside of you. Feel how, through this intermediary, you are linked to all the forces which live in animals, who are themselves the vehicles for the cosmos' soul of desire and feeling.

Think and feel how your astral soul carries all visible and invisible animals. These are influences which live within you and wish to direct your life, to manifest themselves through your being.

The Spiritual Sun of Wisdom and the Vibration of the Corpus Christi

Now concentrate on humanity and its intelligence. Look with the eye of the spirit at how your ability to think is linked to that of humanity, which itself is one with the cosmic intelligence.

Feel how you can unite your thoughts to those of the cosmic intelligence. There is then a light of wisdom which can appear in your thoughts. The wisdom that a disciple can receive in this way does not come from the world or from humanity, but from the cosmic intelligence. Through it, the disciple can harmonize his feelings and direct his life in accordance with the great law of cosmic morality. So the disciple who reaches the spiritual sun of wisdom can restore order within himself and radiate a light that imprints itself on the substance of his life. The light of true wisdom is the consecration which changes the physical man into a true man in the spirit.

The spiritual sun of wisdom carries within itself the image of the true man, which shows the disciple how man should be, how man was conceived by God in perfection and purity.

Next, concentrate on the fact that, in your sphere of thought, you contain all the thoughts of the world. If you do not think in harmony with the image of the solar man that you have just contemplated, you introduce into yourself, and into the thoughts of the world, illness and trouble. On the other hand, if you welcome the light of wisdom of the cosmic intelligence, you bring the blessing of the Holy Spirit upon yourself and upon the world's sphere of thought. This light of wisdom in your thoughts will begin to restore order in your sphere of feelings; and, in this way, you will bring peace and harmony to yourself and to the world.

This mastery of light will imprint itself on the sphere of life, giving birth to a surge of power in the will, a surge towards a new, purer life—harmonious and rejuvenated.

In this way, you will introduce into yourself, and into the world, the vibration of divine life that heals, revitalizes, and breathes life into, the human soul.

This desire for divine life transforms the physical body, making it more capable of receiving and carrying the high vibrations of the divine spirit. It is in this way that you will carry in yourself, and in the world, the vibration of the Corpus Christi, of the body of Christ, of enlightened humanity, of the solar earth.

The Experience of the Hierarchy

Through the hierarchy—minerals, plants, animals, humans, angels, archangels—which makes up the cosmos, the student clearly perceives that what is below supports what is above, all the while striving to rise up towards it. The mineral wants to become a plant, to have the power to transform matter and reproduce. The plant aspires to change into an animal, and so on. This is the direction of life.

What the disciple understands through all these spiritual experiences is that it is the image of the superior which inspires the inferior to evolve. For the mineral, the plant is a real sun, giving it a lesson at certain times of the year. Likewise, the plant receives a lesson from the animal, but also from the sun, which represents its superior self. The animal receives a lesson from the true man—that is, the man who is the carrier of love and wisdom. Man receives a lesson from the superior self which lives and radiates in the world of angels. It was to point out this law that Christ said that his disciples could contemplate the son of man, above whom the angels rise and descend.

Obviously, there is also a hierarchy within each level, which is why, in humanity, some are closer to the world of angels—teachers, servants of enlightened humanity—while others are closer to the human, animal, plant and mineral worlds.

Solar Initiation

Through his contemplation, our student understands that

what the sun is to the plant, the superior self is to man. At night, he sees that his mineral-and-plant body stays in bed while his animal body and his self, which make up his earthly personality, leave it. He then has that troubling experience, so full of meaning, that he is like the sun and the water from the sky for his mineral-and-plant body. Continuing with his esoteric investigation, he perceives that the animal is ruled by urges, emotions and desires which it does not control, whereas if he, as a human being, wants to control his positive and negative forces, he must become stronger and concentrate on the light which lives in his conscious self.

This light allows him to be free, to be the master of his movements and his acts in his astral-animal soul.

Accomplishing this mastery based on a harmonization of the energies, he realizes that, at the same time that he is acquiring a state of serenity in his feelings, he can detach himself from them more and more to become nothing more than a self-awareness. This pure self-awareness, with nothing else mixed in, is linked to the spiritual sun, whereas his animal soul was linked to the moon and the planets.

In having this experience of approaching the source of the conscious self, of the cosmic I-Am, the disciple lives what the ordinary man can only know after his physical death. This is one of the privileges of initiation.

It is very difficult to correctly describe this experience of the life of the soul; but we can say that our student feels cut-off from everything that makes up his false nature, from everything that is mortal and ephemeral. His physical and etheric body lies on his bed; his astral body, his personality, has stayed in the realms of the moon. And he, in the essence of his conscious self, reaches the source of the spiritual sun of the cosmos, which he perceives as being the intimate essence of himself and of everything, the origin of his being and of all beings—that which does not die, but remains unchanged throughout all of the incarnations and cyclic manifestations.

Moses on Mount Sinai and the Meeting with the Angel of Light

The story of Moses climbing Mount Sinai to speak with the Eternal One is a faithful description of what we are explaining here, which was scientifically realized in the initiatic temples of Egypt. Moses climbed the mountain, meaning that he rose up towards the spiritual world. When he reaches the chosen place, he has to take off his shoes because the place is sacred; and indeed, the spiritual sun, the source of the self, is the most sacred place in man.

Over the centuries, millions of disciples and initiates have concentrated on reaching this place, this sanctuary of the true man. This is why Christ said to his disciples through the Master Jesus: *"Search and you will find."* *"But those things about which you questioned me before, and which I did not tell you— today I am ready to reveal them, but you no longer question me."* When Moses stands in this place of the soul, in the right way, the Eternal One himself appears before him: *"I am the I-Am self who speaks to you"*; *"I am he who was, who is, who will be."*

The contemporary student of the Johannite school of the Rose+Cross is led to live an analogous experience; he finds himself in front of an infinite light and, at the same time, he feels that he is living within this light, that it is the source of his life, of his being. He understands that this sun of suns is the cosmic self, the self which is reflected in all selves and which calls all humans to rise up towards it, just as the visible sun calls the plants.

Inside this light, he sees the angelic form of a man of dia-mond-light, of a resplendent god, and understands that this is the only son of the celestial Father, the structure of light of the true man, the perfect model from which all humans were cre-ated, made in the image of God and the cosmos.

It is then that the angelic being speaks. He reveals sublime, magnificent mysteries, which man can only understand when he is in this state of being.

Among other things, he says that he is the true being of the disciple and of all beings, and that, one day, they will fuse to become one in a mystical marriage. But, for the moment, the disciple is not ready; he has more experiences to live on earth—in particular, gaining control of his physical, etheric, astral and mental vehicles, to align them within himself, the divine man.

This is when the Christ-being gives him the initiatic teaching necessary to accomplish his task. Then he approaches the self of the disciple to unite with it in a mystic fusion, through which the disciple can live the state of being of his real being and taste the experience of eternity, of infinity, of the limitless in everything.

He understands why the authentic initiates insisted so much on their teaching "know your own self".

This knowledge of oneself, or of the Self, contains all of the science, wisdom and love of the universe; it is the key to the world of truth. Compared to this living knowledge of the true nature of man, all the rest—all the diplomas and the knowledge of the world—become unreal shadows, empty shells.

The Structure of Light of the Universe and of Man

Our student can then contemplate around the solar man a whole structure of light that is made up of a hierarchy of beings who are his servants in the whole cosmos.

In his gospel, as well as in his Apocalypse, the Master St. John speaks only of these mysteries, and we are unveiling here their quintessence for our time. When he describes the celestial Jerusalem, or the twenty-four wise men who surround the throne of the lamb, he is describing, through symbolic imagery, the hierarchy of spiritual beings who surround and serve the image of the cosmic man, the creative Word. In reality, this is the structure of esoteric light from which man and the cosmos were created. Our student can contemplate all of this by himself when he lives the experiences that we have just described. He sees it, just as an ordinary man can look at a landscape on the earth.

All of this sacred science is conserved intact, pure and alive in the land of Shamballa; and the disciple can contemplate this land of light which surrounds, in a hierarchy, the sun of the divine man.

He understands within himself, through direct perception, all that the great initiates wanted to say through their words, their messages.

For example, when Christ, through the Master Jesus, spoke about the son of man, he was referring to the personality composed of the mineral, plant, animal, and human aspects. This personality is created from the substance radiated by the divine sun, which is the cosmic man, the creative Word, the only son of God. Therefore, all humans, and even all beings, carry within them this only son of God.

When Christ says *"The son of man must become the son of God"*, he is alluding to evolution, ascension, the meaning of life for all beings.

The Grass and the Mysteries of the Akasha Chronica

After contemplating and living all of these mysteries in the spiritual world, our student turns towards the earth; and there he sees his astral body, his sidereal soul. From his point of view, he understands that the astral surrounds the earth and plant life, and that he must go through it again to rejoin his physical body. When he looks at his etheric-physical body, he sees the image of a field covered with grass. These are great mysteries.

He thinks: "The grass contains a memory of light; and, through its exposition to all the angels of the cosmos, it is engraved with all the knowledge of the universe, of the Cosmic Tradition. The grass contains the secrets of the Akasha Chronica and my etheric-physical body also contains them."

Seeing his etheric-physical body as a grassy field, he understands that his body is engraved with, has memorized, universal knowledge, and that it is the astral-mental body, the personality, that stops him from reading this teaching, from remembering. In taking on his personality once again, he will lose the memory of his spiritual experience; and, on earth, he will no longer be able to read the same message in the body. It is then that he perceives that the authentic initiatic schools of the current of St. John possess very powerful spiritual exercises which emanate from the circle of the Masters of the Cosmic Tradition (dances, melodies, sounds, mantric words, ways of life, etc.), whose role is to reveal, in the etheric-physical body of man, the universal knowledge that it contains. (1)

The ancient schools of mysteries symbolized this initiatic level with a cow, then with a bull. In the Apocalypse, this bull is mentioned as one of the four animals surrounding the throne of the lamb; and all of this symbolic language contains the mysteries that we are revealing here.

The ancient initiates had understood perfectly that the cow has a particular rapport with the earth, with grass, and with the mysteries of nutrition and digestion. It is for this reason that they had taken it as the symbol of the first degree of the spiritual development of the disciples.

---

(1) For more information on this subject, consult the internal teachings of the School of Life and Spirit. (Editor's note).

The Image of the Lion and the Secrets of the Guardian of the Threshold

When our student concentrates once again on his astral body, he can see, from a spiritual perspective, the image of a lion. This lion symbolizes the tendencies of the false, egoistical personality. In contemplating it, the disciple understands the words of Christ to his disciples: *"Happy the lion that the man will eat; the lion will become man. Unhappy the man that the lion will eat; the man will become lion!"*

Looking at this lion more closely, he sees it metamorphose into the form of a dark man, half-human and half-animal, and understands that this image is linked to him. It is the sum of all the negative, destructive and anarchic experiences, actions, feelings, and thoughts that he has had in the past. This form links him in a magic way to certain dark places and prevents him from receiving the inspirations of his divine nature, of Christ, of the enlightened man. So man is not really free to choose his destiny, since most of his acts and inner tendencies are determined by his past actions, which are synthesized in the form he is contemplating. This form is the guardian of what is called karma in the tradition of India.

At this stage of spiritual perception, our student finds himself between, on one side, the image of the solar man towards which he is going, and, on the other side, that of his personality, of the ancient man whom he has to transform to be able to unite himself with the light, as he was told by the superior self. One must realize that the disciple would never be able to contemplate this image of his negative karma, of his dark destiny personified, if the vision of the light did not counterbalance its weight and soften it. Without this vision of light of the future being of man, of Christ, the disciple would be lost, destroyed.

Jesus Is Everything to Me

Arriving at this stage of spiritual clairvoyance, the Rose+Cross student understands the words of the Master Christian Rose+Cross: *"Jesus (the man of light) is everything to me."* These mantric words can really only be understood by the students of the Johannite Rose+Cross. Those who pretend to grasp these words without having passed through the phases of initiation that we describe are deluding themselves.

Facing this image of his dark karma, the disciple realizes that he is only able to perceive it like this because it has come out of him, and that he has managed, in a way, to detach himself from it by rising towards the superior self. Before, he did not see it because it was inside him and secretly directed his life. Now he understands that he has become responsible for his life in a higher way because, before, he had created this image unconsciously; but now he must transform it into a being of light, through his model vision of the Johannite man, of enlightened humanity.

The Vision of the Pyramid of Light of Shamballa

If a Johannite student and an ordinary being look together at the space, the atmosphere, the infinity before them in an earthly landscape, they will not have the same perception. The ordinary man will see, more or less, the beauty of the colors, the harmony of the shapes, and the unity, depending on his level of human evolution. The Johannite disciple will perceive the same landscape; but, in the atmosphere, he will see the great pyramid of etheric light of the universal Brotherhood-Sisterhood, and also the column of diamond-light of the holy land—Manisola, Shamballa.

Inside this vision, he will see the spiritual sun of the true man. It is this etheric vision which guides all the initiates and good men of the planet. This etheric vision is clearly described in the bible when a column of fire and a thick cloud guide Moses and the Jewish people. When the disciple turns his back on this spiritual sun of the good and worthy man, of the pure man wanted by God, he sees before him the image of his shadow on the ground, and through it appears the hideous shape which he must transform. In this way, the disciple is guided on his path and cannot, must not, go off of the road. He takes his first steps towards becoming the master of his destiny, knowing that all his thoughts, feelings and acts are seeds planted in the substance of life, and that they carry within them their own development, for which he is, absolutely, the only one responsible. This law applies to everyone, but he has become aware of it. Initiation only elevates and enlarges the consciousness. Our student, while contemplating this dark form, the reflection of his own personality, understands that this is what obliges beings to reincarnate, because, until it has become transparent and pure, man must keep coming back to earth. It is with this form that man must unite with the superior self. To explain this mystery, Christ said: *The kingdom of heaven belongs to those who resemble it.*

Working on the Personality

Standing before the angelic world and the Masters of karma, the lords of destiny and evolution, man can hide nothing; they can read him like an open book. They see this form and know exactly everything he has done, his secret motivations, and the level of the disciple's evolution. Because of this knowledge, they are able to give him the best conditions for his evolution.

When a disciple has finally embellished this form, made it luminous and pure like its solar model, then the powers of death, limitation and evil no longer have any hold on him.

Many people who say they have seen the devil have, in reality, only seen the form of their personality reflected in the astral light. All of the wicked people who, through envy, disappointment or pride, have wanted to make a pact with the devil have, in reality, turned themselves into the devil, have created the devil inside them, and have become him in their personality, by their wicked and criminal desires and acts. The good disciple, who has understood the meaning of life and the meaning of universal love, strives to become an artist to create, in this astral light, a pure, angelic form, woven from the best thoughts and kind acts.

But this form of the personality is not tied only to the disciple; it is attached, in a magical way, to a family tree, a region, a people, a race, a country.

All of these ties, whether we recognize or deny them, are much more powerful than we may think.

When the disciple has attained a certain level of development, he becomes incorporated into the current of St. John, into "this people beyond races and limitations" in the humanity of light; and this is a very important moment in the life of a soul.

The Circle of the Zodiac and the Etheric Body of Man

Our student now concentrates his vision through the astral form of the karmic personality towards his etheric body, which penetrates his physical body; and there he sees what appears to be a circle of light, a circle linked to the cosmos, inside which he can distinguish twelve sources of light. He recognizes the image of the circle of the zodiac in the etheric which surrounds the body and understands that this circle is tied to the great zodiac circle, which contains the whole universe and all of its mysteries.

It is very difficult to describe these realities because they belong to other dimensions and cannot be reduced enough to fit into our language. However, we can say that the disciple sees the son of man, and the angels of the Celestial Father rising and descending above him. This means that he contemplates, in indescribable splendor, how the whole cosmos works and lives in the etheric body of man, to lead him and to help him advance on the path of evolution.

When we speak of the etheric body, we are thinking not only of the force which enlivens the physical body, but also, definitely, of the soul of life.

Now, life is infinite; it is in the physical body, but also in the astral, mental, individual, universal soul. It is in God himself. Life is God acting in the universe, in creation. So, by working on the life within him, on his etheric body, which has the form of the zodiac, the disciple understands that he is working on the Whole. Life is the basis, the foundation, of initiatic work; and it is for this reason that the cabalists call the etheric body Yesod—the foundation.

When the disciple's etheric body is in harmony with that of the cosmos, then the disciple lives in the light of the Cosmic Tradition, and the twenty-four wise men bless him; but, when they are not in harmony, man experiences suffering, sickness and death. We are now going to give some exercises and methods of the Cosmic Tradition for harmonizing the etheric body and for accelerating the harmonious evolution of man and the earth. (1)

Rosicrucian Meditation on the Organs

Behind all of the organs of the body—like the stomach, the heart, the brain—there are intelligent beings, forces which are at work in man, and in constant communion with the cosmos.

---

(1) The author is referring to the twelve movements and visualizations of the etheric dance of the man of light, which he then gave in the workshops of the School of Life and Spirit. (Editor's Note).

Exercise

You can have this free experience. Prepare yourself for meditation.

Concentrate on an organ—for example, the heart.

Move towards it with your thoughts and feel it with your feelings.

Become aware that it lives and works in a way that is independent of your conscious will.

Become aware that, without its work, you could not live on earth. Therefore, there is a force, an energy, an intelligence, which created this heart and united itself to you so that you could live on earth.

Feel the beats of the heart, and the circulation of the blood throughout the whole body.

Feel how all of this work is tied to that of breathing, which also has its own rhythm.

You can now try to feel this rhythm, and this pulsation and purification of life, everywhere in nature and in the cosmos.

In this way, you can tie your heart to the great heart of the universe. Do it.

Now come back to your own heart. Try to feel the vibration of the life that is behind it. Is it the same as the one for the feet or the brain? Feel that.

The one-life of the etheric body specifies itself through the organs of the physical body. For that, it divides itself into twelve, and you can feel these twelve doors forming themselves into a circle of silver light which surrounds your physical body.

The heart is linked to the door of the lion, as the heart of the cosmos is linked to the zodiac constellation of the lion. Try to feel all of this in your meditation. These are the first steps towards a divine, infinite, unknown science.

Man Is a Hieroglyph of the Cosmos

Seeing all of this with spiritual awareness, our student realizes that each man possesses within himself all the wisdom of the cosmos; he understands the words of the Masters of the Cosmic Tradition: *"Man is a hieroglyph of the cosmos."*

In addition, he sees how the soul is linked to the physical body; what projects the cosmic intelligence has for the physical body; how the laws of destiny are elaborated; how, for every new incarnation, a new personality is constructed, based on a recording of the quintessence of the previous one. This karmic recording in the astral light comes from the form, the image of the man, that we spoke about earlier. And the creative force which constructs the body is the etheric body, the zodiac circle that surrounds man and represents the creative power of life. The disciple must transform his astral image; but, also, he must seize the creative power of the zodiac, following the impulse of the superior self in his conscious self. This is the whole secret of initiation.

The Twelve Knights of the Round Table and the Forces of the Zodiac

The sum-total of all of this is that the goal of initiation and of man's life on earth is to contemplate the image of the enlightened man, who is none other than the cosmic Word, and to incarnate it in his flesh. Until man has obtained the vision of the I-Am, of Christ, he cannot accomplish much in life.

The ordinary man gains this knowledge, this vision, between death and a new birth; but, in constructing a new personality, he develops amnesia and identifies with his physical nature. So man loses his free and legitimate creative power, and falls under the blind and fatal influence of the forces which generate the mortal personality.

The knights of the Round Table knew all about these mysteries. This table symbolized the secrets of the etheric body, and the twelve knights those of the zodiac—therefore, those of the macrocosmos and microcosmos, which are tied to it. These twelve signs of the zodiac are a synthesis of all the powers and influences at work in the universe, which, by condensing themselves, created the physical and etheric bodies of man. It is through them that the one, divine, universal and impersonal life constructed time and space, within which nature and the personality move.

The objective of the one-life intelligence is to transform matter into light and to give the light a perfect form; and, for that, it works thousands, even billions, of years.

Man on earth must participate in this work, individually and collectively; one can even say that he is one of the principal tools, because he is responsible for the future evolution of animals, plants and minerals.

These twelve knights of the zodiac, assembled around the Round Table, were waiting for a thirteenth knight—that is to say, the force, the light, of the divine I-Am, of the son of God, of the superior self, which, by appearing in the etheric-physical body of man, allows a new birth, a spiritual awakening, just as the sun makes flowers blossom. The etheric zodiac which constructs the personality and the destiny of man is asleep, even if man gesticulates, speaks, acts; in reality, it is sleeping like the tree in winter. It is not the superior self that constructed the personality and directs the life of man.

When the superior self touches, with its rays, the zodiac circle of man's etheric body, man starts to come to life, to be resurrected, to awaken.

The twelve knights were also looking for the cup of the Holy

Grail, which is formed by the moon at certain periods of its cyclic evolution. This cup represents the mastery and the purification of the astral-mental body of the personality, which allows the light of the Christ-self to show through the personality and to touch the physical and etheric bodies.

Another task of the knights was to fight against the monsters, dragons, and negative forces which cut man off from his true nature, and from his harmonious union with the cosmos and the land of good life. This fight is linked to the purification of the atmosphere of the humanity polluted by certain desires, feelings, and thoughts.

The Disciple Becomes One with the Thirteenth, with the Etheric Body of Christian Rose+Cross

When living these experiences which we have described, in the field of life of the Rose+Cross, the disciple, upon penetrating, once again, his astral soul, felt strongly the necessity to form within himself a pure cup that would be capable of receiving properly the divine Self's impulse of Christ.

Without this cup, the disciple perceived that he was losing the vibratory quality of his luminous experience.

In the same way, when he returned to his etheric-physical body, he clearly felt the twelve cosmic forces of life within him;

and he was the thirteenth, a new impulse to revive and rejuvenate life, to carry it forward on the path of evolution.

He could feel that he was becoming a free creator; but he also perceived that many hostile, opposing forces were still moving in his personality, as well as in the great personality of humanity.

Having arrived at this point of spiritual perception, the disciple is ready to consciously work on, and serve, the great task of the initiates, of the children of light: the realization of the kingdom of God on earth as it is in heaven, the incarnation of the man of light, the construction of the golden temple of the solar culture in humanity.

We are going to try to give some concrete indications for advancing on this path of service and initiation, in accordance with the needs of our times. What we have explained and described here contains a knowledge that is essential for man, and that he must meditate upon and deepen on his own.

These thoughts have the power to open centers of spiritual perceptions in the being who is worthy of them, who reflects on them in a lucid and concrete way.

Peace and freedom to all humans-disciples:
light, love and life.

Know that the authentic Masters
and the guides of humanity were like you,
and that they often become so again
to help their followers.
So your daily life and the circumstances
in which you find yourself are not an obstacle
on the path that leads to our art.

The Meaning of Life

How to Transform Your Life into a Garden of Roses

Official knowledge does not teach the meaning of life, but more the meaning of matter—how to succeed in the world of matter, how to make a success of your material life. Of course, this knowledge is useful from a certain viewpoint; but the knowledge of the meaning of life is something else altogether, and, in order to approach it, one must also study the soul and the spirit of man and of the cosmos in its various manifestations.

By plunging himself solely into the study of the material

world, man finds death, despair, limitation and destruction. By thinking only of material success, of satisfying the needs of the body, man is dragged into a current of death; and that is where one finds the origin of all of the imbalances prevalent today in humans and in societies.

Other teachings which perceived this problem chose to focus on the development of the personality—the power of thought and of the will, the spreading of love, etc.

These are all the techniques that we now find in the "new age". Having understood that the inner life of the personality is an important factor in success, and one which is completely neglected by the official knowledge, they teach how to succeed in one's life; how to improve one's competitiveness, charm, and magnetism; how to create material prosperity; how to gain the trust of other people; how to get ahead in one's job; how to have a successful marriage—in short, how to transform one's life into a garden of roses.

Of course, these "new age" teachers have discovered some truths—notably, the importance of the will; however, in reality, this simply aggravates the situation. A willful personality, cultivating the old selfishness, and putting itself at the service of the great worldly personality—is not that something even more frightening? So one must not be lured into this. This knowledge definitely does not lead to the understanding of the meaning of life.

Those who are able to teach, in truth, how to transform life, humanity, and the earth into a garden of roses, are, precisely, the Rose+Cross, the circle of light of the Masters and guides of humanity. We are going to convey here some information and exercises that the Johannite school teaches to students who wish to progress towards the land of the good life. (1)

The Living Teaching of the Rose+Cross

Above all else, the teaching of the Rose+Cross transmits the Johannite Solar and Cosmic Tradition for the initiatic development of the western world. By Johannite Solar teaching, we mean Christianity in the hidden purity of its divine essence.

The objective of the teaching is the harmonious perfecting of humanity and the embellishment of life. It is absolutely not motivated by selfish, limited preoccupations, but places sacrifice and service for the universal good, for the Whole, before everything else.

It has a love for knowledge and for the science of the spirit, and loves those who aspire to learn in order to carry life to a higher level. It pushes its disciples towards the free and living

---

(1) In all of the works of the author, you will find teachings and exercises which come from the Johannite Rose+Cross. (Editor's note).

experience of the mysteries of life.

The hierophants of the Rose+Cross have always asked their students to not only look at visible forms, but to consider life above everything and to put it first.

For them, understanding the meaning of life is the most important thing for each individual, for every race of people, and for all of humanity, which they consider as a global being.

This knowledge is essential because it is the foundation on which life rests and develops.

If a house has unstable foundations, the whole building threatens to collapse. This is why the meaning of life should be the first thing that is taught to a child on earth, in the bosom of its family, and all through its education, from school to university, for life in society. However, in schools, they are content with superficial knowledge. This knowledge is only interested in the external world. For example, knowing what a stalk, or a grain, of wheat is means having an internal picture showing that it is made up of certain chemical elements which are edible for man; and that is all.

The disciple considers the inner life of the stalk, and comes to the conclusion that the grain of wheat is the quintessence of the whole plant and that it carries within it the life that can form a new stalk. So the disciple enters into contact with the internal life of the stalk of wheat; and it is life itself that teaches him by touching his own life in some way.

The Grain of Wheat and Reincarnation

It is a fact that the grain of wheat has certain nutritive qualities, but that is not what interests it; that is not the goal of its life.

Therefore, the grain of wheat can teach man that what is important is not only the external qualities, but the life which will flow from everything that man carries within him. A man's head could be compared to the grain of wheat. Man gains a knowledge of the world through all of the experiences he has in life, just as the stalk forms the grain of wheat. But the most important thing is not the knowledge itself; it is, rather, the life that it holds for the future man, the new man of light.

By meditating on a stalk of wheat, the disciple can uncover secrets about the transmigration of souls from one incarnation to another, and about the meaning of evolution. He can understand how to develop within himself forces of life which will help to transform him in the direction of greater perfection, just as man can improve the qualities of plants through various types of cross-breeding and grafting.

If man does not know the meaning of life, he unites himself to a current of death; and, in his next incarnation, he will be born with diminished capacities. All the external knowledge which is stuffed into humanity these days will not be passed on from one incarnation to another, because, in his essential being, man does not need this, just as the grain of wheat does not need to know that it possesses nutritive elements for man.

The only knowledge that is important for man is the one that allows him to become perfect and to find eternity.

The Harmony Between Internal and External Knowledge

External knowledge is abusive and drains man of his internal life; it annihilates his capacity to acquire the wisdom born of spiritual experience.

So we are moving towards a degeneration of humanity.

What good is extensive knowledge if, from it, we cannot draw anything for our internal and spiritual evolution, if we are incapable of transforming it into the delectable fruit that brings life and happiness to others?

Ignorant of the meaning of life, man has developed the technique for devaluing life, and thereby increasing death.

We do not mean that external knowledge is essentially bad; but, in everything, harmony must reign. Man has to understand that everything he does must be useful for the spiritual world, for the Whole; and he must offer his knowledge to the Divine, just as the Divine, the Whole, offers him life and Everything possible. This is the harmonious exchange.

One must not acquire knowledge just for the sake of knowlcdge, but to evolve in one's own initiation, and to offer it to, and put it at the service of, the universal community. By doing this, by cultivating this state of consciousness and of life, man is not distanced, or cut off, from the sacred current of divine evolution. This is a great challenge for our era—consciously uniting external knowledge with the internal knowledge of the awakened human soul.

Those who practice this divine service with humility and perseverance will bring a healing balm to all of humanity, to the earth, to the spirits of nature and of the elements, and to all sick angels.

What science discovers in the outside world can be tied in with, and become a key for, inner knowledge. Christ worked hard to establish this tie during his incarnation in the Master Jesus, and this is why he often spoke in parables. He used an example from everyday life to teach a divine initiatic lesson which encourages man to move forward in the current of life. In the same way, the Rose+Cross has worked to unite scientific experience with the internal evolution of the soul.

An Exercise of the Brothers and Sisters of the Rose+Cross

If you wish to participate in this work, you can start by practicing this exercise in the mornings.

Relax, breathe deeply and harmoniously, and enter your inner being.

Think: "All of the experiences, the impressions, and the representations—whatever they may be—that I will be led to have today, I offer to the divine world, and to Christ so that his kingdom may come to earth."

Do the same thing at night, offering all you have learned during the day to the world of light.

You must only offer external knowledge, which you were not able to, or did not know how to, transform into spiritual experiences, into the light of wisdom.

You can practice this exercise until it becomes a good habit, awakened and living, to send the surplus of knowledge and experiences towards the beings of light who know how to use them, in the same way that man knows how to utilize the grain of wheat that has not been planted in the earth—he transforms it into food. To take a grain of wheat out of the ground just to deliberately let it rot is really not a good thing. Likewise, we must not take knowledge and symbols from the etheric world without extracting something spiritual from them, or sending them towards the luminous angels who will know what to do with them. This is a great cause of sickness in our era, which is rich in useless information, and which pillages and hijacks the subtle and divine energies.

May all those who sincerely practice this Rose+Cross exercise receive our blessing of light and our encouragement.

The Etheric Force of Sacred Service

If, in the schools of the ancient mysteries, initiatic knowledge was taught under the seal of secrecy, it was to ensure that the candidate would preserve as sacred the precious gift which he received. They had to be sure that the inner life was not separated from the divine knowledge; the evolution of humanity was dependent on this, and it still is today.

Just the fact of receiving this initiatic teaching should be considered by the disciple as a blessing from heaven, and the possibility of being the bearer of it as a true cosmic service for God.

If you really want to become a student of the Johannite humanity, of the circle of Masters of the Rose+Cross, you must acquire, and cultivate in a new way, the sensitivity and the special feelings which can be born in the soul of the one who understands what we have just said and who wishes to participate in this kind of sacred service.

The one who performs this service will radiate etheric forces of light which will heal and harmonize the etheric of humanity and of all the sick beings on earth. This will happen naturally, without the disciple even realizing it.

The Law of the Cosmic Economy

This basic exercise of the Rose+Cross current contains a formidable teaching which we will not develop further for the moment; but we will point it out anyway, for those who would like to go into it more deeply. It contains the secret of the true cosmic economy. In nature, everything is counted and used in the proper way. The cosmic intelligence is aware of the smallest speck of dust flying through the air, of the tiniest thought; and it recognizes its usefulness, its role. For it, the idea of waste, or of deficit, is unknown. Man must follow this example, and finally understand that he must put the divine first, so that everything else revolves around it, and is linked to it in one way or another. In this way, no energy is lost. All of those spiritual energies diverted from their original function to serve only ephemeral things become the greatest source of illness and suffering for humanity.

There is a whole sensitivity, a whole state of consciousness, to be found.

The one who understands the meaning of divine evolution sees that everything comes from the source of life, behind which is the divine intelligence, and that everything returns to it.

Therefore, everything belongs to God; and man does not own the earth, or anything else.

Things have been put into his hands and he is responsible for them, because, one day, the accounts will be settled.

The task of a disciple is to make the sacred treasure of the Eternal bear fruit; in this way, he can continually make progress. The others—the materialists, et al—are moving towards degeneration, towards spiritual, moral, intellectual, and even material, impoverishment.

Let's suppose that a man is rich and that he lives solely for the pleasure of the senses, of selfish satisfaction, of debauchery and intrigue. Not only will he be poor in his next incarnation, and will he not even remember that he was rich and powerful before. The worst thing is that he will be equally poor spiritually, intellectually and morally.

The one who is spiritually rich possesses all the treasures of the world.

Basic Exercise of the Rose+Cross Current

Go to the place consecrated to your spiritual work, and find the correct position and attitude, following the instructions of the School of Life and Spirit.

Breathe calmly and deeply, and let all of your personal problems gently fade away.

You find yourself in a state of silent awakening.

Consciously think: LIFE – LIFE – LIFE...

Be relaxed, but do not allow any other thought to enter you.

If you feel that you have strayed from your concentration, consciously say the word LIFE, and then go back to your mental concentration.

Do not be discouraged if you have trouble concentrating on this simple thought; that it is quite normal. You must simply persevere harmoniously in this exercise, because the fact that you feel some resistance shows that you need it urgently, that it is vital for you. You will see your life improve as a result of it.

When you feel that your mental concentration is synchronized with the conscious thought, you can begin to try to see where that thought is situated. Is it in the feet, the stomach, the thorax or the head? When you have found the place, without losing your concentration, you can try to enlarge the perception of the thought throughout the whole body.

The synchronization between the mental concentration and the conscious thought can be attained when the internal pronunciation is in harmony with the respiratory rhythm. See how the respiratory rhythm brings another quality to the pronunciation.

You can also make another discovery if you touch the center of the abdomen, seat of the will, with your deep and gentle breathing.

When only in the head, the thought was abstract; in the respiratory system, it takes on an inner feeling, and, in the abdomen, it moves, comes to life and gains energy.

When you have succeeded in enlarging and controlling the thought throughout the whole body, you can have this experience of imagining it in front of you, in front of your face. Look, try to see this thought in front of your face.

When you have obtained this perception of the thought, continue to concentrate on it; and, at the same time, ask yourself: is this thought in accordance with, is it an exact representation of, life in its universal reality? Then you must erase the thought that you have formed in the space in front of you and allow to come into its place, into the emptiness thus created, the vision, the perception, of universal life.

Of course, this exercise must be broken up in its realization; you must proceed in stages, until the moment when you are able to do it in its entirety.

It is also important not to ask oneself questions about life during the mental concentration. One must go from the vision of the thought, thus created, to the direct perception of universal life in its essence, without any intermediary. This is an intuitive perception, which must go beyond the perception of the personality that thinks, feels and wants.

The Direct Perception of the One-Life

When the disciple has obtained this vision of the one-life—of impersonal, universal life—an alliance of light is then formed between him and it; and he starts to see life in all of its different manifestations. He realizes that everything is full of life and intelligence. He sees things that we cannot describe, because what is normally invisible to modern man becomes visible to him. In fact, to concentrate on life and to put it first is to learn to perceive what is invisible.

For example, a man sees a very pretty girl, with a lovely figure, and he is attracted to her. The disciple also finds the girl pretty; but, when he perceives the life around her, the dark vibrations that she gives off, he is not attracted to her, because he sees clearly that her life is not intense, pure and divine. Only divine life leads to a full and abundant life.

In the same way, the official scientific mentality sees no difference between two thinking men.

It is able to describe wonderfully all of the processes—physiological, biological, electromagnetic—of a thinking man; but its analysis stops there. The disciple, however, sees that one is thinking about killing his wife, while the other one is thinking about how he can help humanity. Even if the physical process for these two trains of thought is the same, the perception of life tells us something completely different.

Looking at two human beings, the disciple can also see a great difference between a thick-headed brute and a learned man. These two men do not serve the energy of the one-life in the same way and with the same goals. The brutish man uses the energy on the mineral-human level, and the learned man on the human level. But the learned man can have a selfish interest and work only for the improvement of material life. There is, therefore, a great difference between this type of learned man and an initiate who has entered the kingdom of the spiritual man.

The spiritual man no longer diverts the energy of life, but works in cosmic unison, in the direction of universal life. He becomes a center of luminous rays, a station for the transformation of life, projecting emanations and forces which radiate very far into the future of humanity. So the spiritual man becomes a conscious creator, a partner in the cosmic work. Through his thoughts, and the three mastered centers of his personality, he is able to create spiritual beings who will take part in the healthy and harmonious evolution.

This involves becoming aware that every human being continually creates forms and beings which will influence his future, his destiny. The difference between ordinary humanity and the initiated disciple is that the disciple breeds them consciously, to unite his life and his destiny to that of the cosmos, to the one which conforms to the will of the Most-High.

The Great Fellowship of Life

Everything that we relate here could be considered as a philosophical theory, and maybe that's true for some people; but one must accept that, for the trained disciple, all of this is a living reality. So when he looks at universal, undifferentiated life, in the air or in the atmosphere, he understands that it is the origin of everything. When this one-life enters his personality, it becomes personal. In his will, it is transformed into movement; in his feelings, into warmth; in his thoughts, into light; in his intelligence, into wisdom.

When he looks at stones, he sees life in all of its degrees, but developed in different ways. Mineral life is more developed in the divine world than in the material world. In the physical, he can perceive a light around the mineral. The stone is a condensation of the one-life which offers itself as a base for the elaboration of a manifestation that is more complex from a material point of view—the plant. Then plant life transforms itself into animal life, and, finally, into human life. In man, life becomes aware of itself.

Therefore, he who learns to perceive life will discover that all beings are related, and, above all, that there is a great fellowship, and even a Brotherhood-Sisterhood, between all of the evolving kingdoms. It will become evident to him that the one-life does not manifest itself in the same way in the mineral, the plant, the animal, the human, the angel; but he understands that the meaning of life emanates precisely from this difference and from this evolutionary will for perfection on the part of the mineral, which becomes a plant, and so on.

The Rose+Cross Concept of the "Celestine" Contains the Meaning of Evolution

The meaning of life is contained in this great law of evolution; and this clarifies the words of Christ to his disciples: *"Be perfect, as the Heavenly Father is perfect"* or *"Look first for the kingdom of heaven, and everything else will be given to you in addition."*

Similarly, when looking at humans, one can notice that there is a great difference between them, in their way of manifesting life. For some, it seems to be mineralized, and one hears people say that they are "thick-headed brutes". Others are plant-like, and it is said that they are vegetating. Others are dominated by their passions, their instincts, and their emotions and one hears about animalistic impulses; while others are thinkers, humanists. It is also said that someone is like an angel.

Even among humans, there is a great difference in the elevation of life. He who honestly knows how to take his place within this classification, and who wishes to rise a degree higher, has understood the meaning of life; he is on the path of enrichment, of ascending evolution.

With Darwin's law, the materialistic scientists repeat endlessly that man comes from the monkey. Instead of being ecstatic and filled with wonder at such a prodigious evolution, it is as if they are doing everything possible to go back to that level. Despite all of the discoveries, they do not understand that the meaning of life lies in the internal elaboration of a new type of man: the homo-angelus, the man-angel, the "Celestine" of the Rose✝Cross.

The Right Direction and the Opening of the Causal Body

Life gives an impulse for evolution in all beings; but the impulse is not enough for man because it is he himself who, through his conscious thought and his ability to reason, must find and give the right direction. If man does not understand the meaning of life, he chooses the wrong direction and fails. It is the role of the authentic initiatic schools to indicate the right direction on earth; but only to indicate, because it is up to man to understand it by himself and to start on his way.

For the mineral, the direction is indicated by the plant; for the plant, by the animal; for the animal, by man; and for man, by the Master of light, whose highest incarnation on earth is the Master Jesus.

It is for this reason that Christian Rose+Cross, the Master of our sacred and venerable order, spoke the mantra : *"Jesus is everything to me."* A mineral could have said: "The plant is everything to me."

Jesus, incarnating the I-Am Christ on earth, is a divine model of future man. Every human being already carries within him this future man. Christian Rose+Cross gives the name of Jesus to the spiritual and etheric image of the man of light, the "Celestine" who lives within his soul.

When the disciple looks at life and sees the image of the celestial man, he finds that it resembles the one manifested by Christ on earth through the Master Jesus.

Nothing is more beautiful in the life of a man or a woman than the image of the Celestine which engraves itself in their aura, in their sphere of life, and begins to radiate throughout the whole personality. The direction is found, Christ is perceived and recognized internally; the causal body is open and working.

The Causal Aura Is the Master of Destiny

For the person who can see life moving, each being is surrounded by a light that shows his state of consciousness and
his level on the ladder of life. Everyone sees the manifestation
of the mineral, which corresponds to the physical body of man.
Then comes the plant radiance, the etheric body which surrounds the physical body and which is very easy to perceive.
Next, the animal aura, which corresponds to the astral body;
and, finally, the mental aura, which is integrated into the kingdom of humanity. The causal aura surrounds the purely
human state of consciousness and of life, and allows man,
when he awakens, to penetrate the spiritual worlds.

It is what establishes the ties between man and the cosmos.
It is also the Master of destiny and the guardian of karma.

When the image of the man of light appears in the vital
causal aura, it means that the disciple has found the path
towards the light. His destiny is no longer unconscious; the
right direction has been given and received.

The disciple must recognize this image of his superior
nature, accept it, and decide to serve it with all of the forces and
the means of his personality. If he does that, then he will meet
us; he will find the path to the divine school. This work is carried out with the one goal of indicating, and allowing each
seeker to walk freely on, this path.

The Image of the Divine Man as a Spiritual Guide

When Christian Rose+Cross says: *"Jesus is everything to me"*, this is absolutely not an emotion or a horizontal, religious, mystical fervor, but, rather, the description of a fact from a concrete initiatic science which is understood by anyone who has the perception of universal life.

When the disciple sees this image appear in his aura, he notices that his life changes, that everything is transformed in his circle of life; he is guided by the light towards the light.

The disciple understands that he has become a "christophoros", a carrier of the image of the true man wanted by God.

The universal Brotherhood-Sisterhood, the hierarchy of Christ, considers man from on high; and; depending on the vibrations and the emanations which come from him, it places him in one category or another. When the image of the man of light appears in the aura of a being, the universal Brotherhood-Sisterhood understands that he is ready to become a disciple, because he has perceived and recognized the true reality of Christ and he is ready to walk on the path to perfection.

When it is said that man is made in the image of God, it is to indicate the science that we are describing here. But the man-personality has lost the vision and the vibration of this image of his divine reality. However, it continues to live inside him, it is present in his subconscious; and it is the first task of a disciple to take care of this image—to find it and to serve it.

When the man-personality is no longer directed or inspired by this image, he is lost, and his life no longer has any meaning; he is walking in darkness and could fall into the abyss. This image is the sun and human destiny.

The Exercise of the Future Man

In the morning, choose a moment between sunrise and ten o'clock, and position yourself facing the sun. There, in the silence, prepare yourself for the spiritual work.

Really feel your sphere of breathing, calm and harmonious.

Awaken yourself in your consciousness.

Contemplate the sun (1) and tell yourself, try to feel, that you are facing the best representation of your superior self, of your being, and of the true being of all beings.

Through the sun, imagine a perfect man, embodying all of

---

(1) Author's and Editor's warning: This exercise should not involve staring at the sun, but, at most, stealing a glance at the sun for 1/10 of a second, when the sun is close to the horizon. Do not stare at the sun because you will damage your retina. It is an inner contemplation which is required here.

the virtues and qualities of God and of the hierarchy of his servants. Let this solar man come towards you through space.

The closer he gets, the more you feel that he is imprinting himself on your aura, your atmosphere, your thoughts, feelings and will. Let him approach you and penetrate you. Then let him go back into the sun.

End your work and go back to your activities—joyous, serene, and with a clear mind, telling yourself inwardly that you have met your future being.

The Exercise of the Eternal Man

While reflecting and concentrating, you can perceive that man does not live only in the present, but also in the past and the future. There are people who love to talk incessantly about their past; and there are others who are always worrying about their future, or making plans for it.

After preparing yourself in the spiritual work, notice how, with your thoughts, you can plunge yourself into the past, or into the near future.

Notice that, during this projection, you can feel impressions, gain knowledge, have an experience, and bring something back from it into the present. For example, if you concentrate on something sad in the past or in the future, that can give birth to a state of sadness in your soul in the present.

Now expand your past, back to the origin of your being—that is to say, the image of God, the model on which you were created.

If you succeed in reaching this image, you will perceive that it has also expanded your horizon and your future, and that it gives a direction for the present.

Now, in the silence and serenity of your meditation, consciously project yourself into the most distant future, in which you will fuse with the divine man, the son of God.

Imagine a string of golden light which starts from the bridge of your nose and extends through future time and space, maybe through thousands of incarnations, to reach the image of the perfect man. Notice how, being outside of time and space, you can already taste this favorable reality and live it inside yourself as a state of consciousness.

So man can live on earth, but, inside himself, he has the capability to taste the celestial life which awaits him in thousands of years. And this modifies his present; it orients him in the direction of divine life, of the real and pure life.

All of this is mathematical; it is the application of the great laws which govern the cosmos.

The Appearance of Christ in the Etheric of Man

In order to become an awakened Master and creator in the present, the disciple must know the image of the divine man that he will be one day. Man can live the reality of this image from the inside by projecting his consciousness towards the future. In this way, he will be able to say, like Christian Rose+Cross: *"Jesus is everything to me."* Then he will understand that the Rose+Cross exercises which we are going to convey are ways of seizing the great magical agent, the forces and currents of energies which are continuously elaborating the personality, in order to consciously direct them and to hasten the realization of the divine image in oneself and in humanity.

This experience, which consists of contemplating in the etheric, in the energy of life, the image of the future solar man, was described not only by Christian Rose+Cross, but also by St. Paul, who, while walking on the road to Damascus, saw a light come down from the sky, surround him with its brilliance, and speak to him. Similarly, the Master St. John says in his Apocalypse that Christ will appear in the clouds and that those who fought against him will lament their fate. Those who have fought against the image of the true, good, and worthy man will have sown, in their own fields and in the fields of others, the bad seeds of the man with no future; and they will have to pay the just consequences of their acts, words and thoughts. This is what we call karma.

The exercises given throughout this work allow the sincere disciple to transform the unavoidable law of karma and to create a luminous future for himself, by the accumulation of good vibrations, thoughts, words and acts which conform to the healthy and harmonious evolution of humanity.

We insist on all of this because it is essential that the disciple who aspires to practice should possess a state of the truest possible consciousness of the energies that he is going to manipulate and put to use for the purposes of good.

St. John the Baptist also described the experience where he saw the man of light coming towards him from the opposite bank of the river, and he said: *"There is the lamb of God, who takes away the sins of the world..."*, *"He must increase and I must decrease."*

Until man possesses this inner vision of the future man of light, he can only live in continual sin because his life has no meaning. But when he sees the apparition and he recognizes it, his life has meaning once again; and sins and karma disappear. The false personality of the disciple must progressively disappear to leave its place to the true being of man.

It must be understood that, through his thoughts, his feelings and his acts, man is constantly leaving an imprint on the etheric substance of life, and continually creating, in his atmosphere, a world in his image, full of all of the emanations coming from the impulses of his desires and passions of the moment. These emanations acquire a life of their own, more or less powerful according to the intensity of the emission, and are able to act, in turn, on man and humanity.

This is what is called karma or destiny. Until man is united with, and directed by, his Celestine, the image of the divine man, he is dominated by the fatal forces thus created, and he has lost the path to his true destiny, as desired by God.

Knowing and meditating on these sacred laws, the disciple learns to willingly create, on his own, the impulses that will lead him towards true happiness and supreme bliss.

Jesus mili omnia

About the author

Olivier Manitara is a free spiritual teacher. Although he is self-taught, his work is part of an ancestral tradition of light. Born in France in 1964, he began, at a very young age, to instinctively practice exercises which would later prove to be spiritual in nature; he experienced his very first illumination at the age of 12.

At 19, he found himself at a turning point in his life and met a Master who gave a definitive direction to his work.

In 1987, after a period of following several teachings, he decided to go on a three-year retreat, part of which was spent in the mountains of Montsegur in the French Pyrenees.

During this retreat, he developed a program of intensive activities in order to achieve his inner goal.

As a result of the intense experiences which he had undergone, he decided to devote himself entirely to the awakening of the human consciousness, and to freedom.

In 1991, he founded an initiatic School within the current of St. John; and there he began to develop a considerable body of work, giving hundreds of conferences and informal talks. His teaching is also developed through the means of silence, the spoken word, meditation, dances, movements, exercises, songs, etc.—thus renewing the eternal tradition of light which has been guiding humanity since the beginning of time.

He defines himself as a simple man and a technician.

All of the works and teachings that he transmits emanate from this ancestral tradition of light, which belongs to all human beings. They constitute the true roots and origins of every individual and of all peoples, and their one goal is the healthy, harmonious, free and dignified development of humanity and of the earth.

Olivier Manitara received his own training during many years of apprenticeship within the bosom of this tradition, which has remained pure in certain places on the earth. Johannite Christianity opened up to him the door to the source of all of the traditions of all peoples.

He believes that all cultures and teachings emanate from a single, unique source, and that their goal is the ennoblement of man within the light of his true being, so that he may learn how to live his passage upon the earth in a just, full, enriching and beneficial manner.

Everything that he transmits comes from a light which desires to circulate freely from one being towards another, in order to unify them within the higher concept of a Brotherhood-Sisterhood which rises above the selfishness of groups and unites men in simplicity, love, and free communal work. This teaching offers powerful, time-tested tools which allow man to improve life in every area—material as well as spiritual. Its foundation is based upon the greatest simplicity; and it has been deeply experienced and brought to life before being transmitted.

Only someone who deeply experiences all of these things himself can transmit them in a just, simple, authentic and caring way.

This book is published to help promote the free and healthy evolution of man and of the earth and to make possible a luminous and dignified path for humanity.

If you have felt the depth of its teachings, and if you have been touched by its message, you may wish to receive the teachings-by-correspondence given by Olivier Manitara.

These are presented in the form of a booklet and are sent out on the 15th of each month.

These booklets present a teaching that is profoundly initiatic and liberating. It emanates from an ancestral Tradition of light which belongs to all human beings. It constitutes the true roots and origins of every individual and of all peoples; and its goal is the physical and spiritual blossoming—healthy, harmonious, free and dignified—of humanity and of the earth.

These are not just empty words, because this teaching is real, extremely practical, and complete—including a great number of tools, explanations and keys, to enable you to work on yourself, and to take your life and your destiny into your own hands.

Nothing is taught that has not been experienced, brought to life, and truly lived beforehand. Since this teaching is progressive, each person can take from it what he feels he needs at that time.

These confidential booklets contain exercises, secret techniques, essences of meditations, and teachings—to help you face the difficulties of life and of the spiritual path. This is a veritable training-course, which guides the candidate inside his own temple.

In addition, you will receive spiritual assistance, which will help you in your development, because no one can flourish all alone; even the seeds of the greatest trees need the earth, water, air and light to grow.

The School of life possesses an aura of light which can give new life to the sincere seeker and lead him towards the goal.

For any additional information, we remain entirely at your service.

Telesma-Evida
P.O. Box 174, Ahuntsic
Montreal (Qc) H3L 3N7, Canada

Email: telesma.publishing@telesma-evida.com

Visit our web site at
http://www.telesma-evida.com/en/publishing.htm

Books by Olivier Manitara
Available at fine bookstores
or order from Telesma-Evida

THE ESSENES

From Jesus To Our Time

Since the archaeological discovery of the Dead Sea Scrolls in 1946, the word "Essene" has made its way around the world—often raising a lot of questions. Many people were astonished to discover that, two thousand years ago, a brotherhood of holy men, living together in a community, carried within themselves all of the seeds of Christianity and of future western civilization. This brotherhood—more or less persecuted and ostracized—would bring forth people who would change the face of the world and the course of history. Indeed, almost all of the principal founders of what would later be called Christianity were Essenes—St. Ann, Joseph and Mary, John the Baptist, Jesus, John the Evangelist, etc.

PEACE

New Method, New Light

Everyone wants peace; yet, there have never been so many wars—at every level of life.

Every day, more and more individuals are taken over—in spite of themselves—by the vibration of anger, of irritability, and of the great conflict pitting everyone against everyone else. Here, the author presents a new and surprising point of view, while revealing methods which become evident, and whose effectiveness is assured for the triumph of peace— both internal and external.

"Peace exists inside every person, and it is up to us to make it flow freely, so that it can illuminate life with its presence, and give us the strength necessary to triumph over all obstacles."

A teaching of a rare quality, dedicated to all those who thirst for peace, justice, light and love—and who are, above all, ready to take action.

CONCENTRATION
ATTENTION
AWAKENING

Their Application in Life

Concentration, attention, and the aspiration to awaken to a higher consciousness are three fundamental qualities for anyone who wishes to walk on the path towards uniting his Spirit with the Great Divine Spirit which embraces everything.

Through clear explanations which go straight to the heart of what is most essential, the author conveys a practical teaching—one which has been lived—on these three virtues which allow every person to undertake anything and to succeed in everything.

A book that is unique in its field.
A major key to a better life.

COSMOGONY OF
THE ROSE+CROSS

Message for a Humanity of Light

A superb work which allows us to penetrate into the heart of the most ancient Brotherhood-Sisterhood of love in the world.

The author received the revelation of this cosmogony during a mystical experience, and he takes us along with him, from the dawn of humanity right up to the present time.

This is another way of looking at history. Here, we will discover the creation of the world by the mysterious influences of fear and the description of an ancestral conflict pitting the darkness against the light.

What is so intriguing is that, as we go through these pages, we realize that the story becomes joined to our own lives; it illuminates, harmonizes, and reveals invisible influences which govern the destiny of every person.

This leads to a profound and rare teaching which demonstrates that the Rose+Cross is eternal and that today, just as in the past, it guides man towards what is essential.

Brotherhood-Sisterhood Press offers to all of its customers and friends who have bought this book a Cabalistic Oracle, formed by a numerical method for calculating the individual numbers which serve to determine the character, the temperament and the aptitudes of a person.

A very practical method which is very simple to use, and which gives immediate results.

This offer is entirely free of charge, and is for any person who buys this book; so be sure to take advantage of it!

Just send your request to Telesma-Evida, indicating your name and address. We will then send you your cabalistic method.

Québec, Canada
1999